Praise for ***The Opti***

"This book goes to the heart of the matter; it's a pers...
to cultivate and create the life of your dreams. In a world where so many people have given up and live by default, this book is a breath of fresh air and a beacon of hope. If you're ready to change your life and own your future, you need this book. Well done, Robin!"

—Laurie Buehler-Hamilton, Author of *Living Your Inspired Life: Revealing the Inner Blueprint for Wellness, Balance & Success*

"This book will help you give up the futile and negative patterns of your past and provide you with clear and actionable steps to create a new future."

—Seconde Nimenya, Author of *Evolving Through Adversity*

"A book for our times: fresh, inspiring, and straightforward. When it comes to creating actual positive change in your life, Robin O'Grady hits the nail on the head."

—Laurel Winston, Author of *Carrots Grow From Carrot Seeds: Cultivating 21st Century Customer Service*

"This is the most powerful and practical book about creating the life of your dreams you will ever read! It's loaded with ideas, insights, and hands-on exercises that will change your thinking and results forever."

—Moreah Love, Author of *Becoming the Change You Want to See, A Guidebook: Helping You Transform Your Thoughts for Lasting Results*

"In this life changing book, you will learn how to transform your negative thinking to change your life dramatically. By using these proven principles, Robin O'Grady transformed her life and went from zero to shero and you can too."

—**Al Foxx, Author of** *Achieving No Limits with Attitude Power*

"Want more of the good stuff in your life: joy, love, health, money, and time? This book is the ticket!"

—**Mary West, Author of** *Networking Your Way to Wealth*

"*The Optimist's Edge* is pure personal power. It can change your life."

—**Lisa Sullivan, Author of** *The Boyfriend Tour*

"Robin O'Grady is an inspiration! Her inclusive approach motivates, enlightens, and fully engages her audience. I've seen and heard many speakers but none as dynamic as Robin O'Grady."

—**Sandra Hixson-Matthews, Author of** *Kiss Your Food*

"Robin's book is a gift. If you are finally ready to make positive changes in your life, this book is a must read!"

—**Patrick Snow, International Bestselling Author of** *Creating Your Own Destiny* **and** *The Affluent Entrepreneur*

"Congratulations on making a difficult process not only easy but also inspiring. Robin understands it because she has lived it."

—**Moreah Veston, Author of** *Pleasures and Ponderings: From Nun to Nudist to Now*

"This book is a toolbox. Get rid of your old tools and pick up this book."

—Carol Paul, Author of *Team Clean*

"This book is the joyful guide to change. Robin O'Grady's gift is in her ability to help you turn your coal to diamonds and she freely shares her own journey from adversity to wellbeing along the way."

—Bonnie Richter, Vice President of Winners Don't Quit Association

"Robin's twenty-five year career in human services and her personal experiences have made her an expert and an inspiration. Kudos, Robin! What you've done is nothing short of miraculous!"

—Lori Tsugawa Whaley, Inspirational Speaker

"The Five Star Success System that Robin has created gives you a clear and uncluttered path to greatness. You will indeed be inspired and climb to new heights when you follow her lead. Five Stars for Robin!"

—Brenda Wilewski, Author of *Evolving Your Leadership Style*

"Robin has an amazing story. Her life is a reflection of who she is. Read this book and become all you can be!"

—H.C. Joe Raymond, Personal Coach and Author of *Embracing Change from the Inside Out*

"Robin understands that the thing that deters most people from succeeding is the negative regurgitation of their stories getting in the way of positive action. If this is you, you owe it to yourself to read this book."

—B. Imei Hsu, Licensed Mental Health Counselor

"For the reader who wants to get more joy out of his or her every-day existence and feel a purpose and passion about life, this book is invaluable. Whether it's negative thinking, limiting beliefs, or negative self-talk, without the tools and techniques needed to make the changes, it's easy to stay stuck. *The Optimist's Edge* offers a way to move forward."

—Tyler R. Tichelaar, Ph.D. and
Award-Winning Author of ***The Best Place***

"In this book, author Robin O'Grady shares the valuable lessons she has learned and strategies she has discovered and practiced to create the life of her dreams, and she can help you do the same. She weaves her own personal stories and struggles eloquently throughout the book, illustrating a unique perspective from which she draws to help the reader feel empowered with the ability to change. I especially liked the exercises she included throughout the book. They are easy to complete and designed to cultivate positive changes in very practical ways. What an inspirational book and a great motivator for change!"

—Laura Rude, Author of ***Creating Postpartum Wellness***

The Optimist's Edge

Moving Beyond Negativity to Create Your Amazing Life

Robin O'Grady

Published by Aviva Publishing. Published simultaneously in Canada.

Lake Placid, NY

518-523-1320
www.avivapubs.com

Requests to the Publisher for permission should be addressed to:
The Optimist's Edge
P.O. Box 24, Port Orchard, WA 98366
robinogrady@wavecable.com

Library of Congress Cataloging-in-Publication Data: O'Grady, Robin 1964

The optimist's edge: moving beyond negativity to create your amazing life/ by Robin O'Grady. p. cm.

ISBN: 978-1-938686-78-8

1. Self-actualization (Psychology). 2. Self-realization. 3. Job Satisfaction 4. Success.

I. Title

BF637.S4S654 2013

650.1-dc22
2010003216

Printed in the United States of America10 9 8 7 6 5 4 3 2 1

Dedication

To Craig, Diane, Hillary, Kiara, and Suzanne (names have been changed to protect anonymity), thank you for your humble and quiet examples of hope, selflessness, and love. You will always be alive in my heart, and I thank you for teaching me the greatest lessons I have learned so far.

To my mother, Diana, who taught me by example to be strong, never to give up, and always to extend a hand to others along the way. This book is for you.

With all my love,

Robin O'Grady

Acknowledgments

Thank you to my beloved husband, Fred O'Grady, who has supported my dream from the beginning as I have gone through the process of change and the literal creation of my own amazing life. You are the wind beneath my wings and my best friend, and that you believe in me is the biggest gift of all. I love you....

Thank you to my sons, Jesse and Gavin. You have helped me stretch and grow in ways I never could have anticipated. You have taught me to love fiercely and unconditionally and have made me a better person. You are the very light of my life. Follow your dreams, boys...your lives are your own to create. I am blessed to be your mom.

Thank you to the amazing survivors (now thrivers!) on the *Titanic* that was once our lives: my mother and biggest cheerleader Diana; my sister and my rock, Stephanie, who has built a successful business and raised two beautiful young ladies on her own (you are and always have been my shero); and to my amazing brothers, Brooks and Jeff, who have grown up to be the best family men I know. You have all blessed my life with your love and support, and

I am so grateful for you. Despite our geographical distance, you are always close to my heart.

Thank you to my father and hero, Bob Lund, for always believing in me, especially when I wasn't capable of believing in myself. Your example of personal and professional morals and values and of unconditional love have been a beacon and motivator for me in my own life.

Thank you to my grandparents, who still live on in my heart. Your examples shaped my life, your love provided light in the darkness, and your memory reminds me always of what is most important.

Thank you to the O'Grady and Fields families for loving me and supporting my dream. Your amazing journeys are proof that blood is thicker than water.

Thank you to the professional, fearless, and joyful team of servant leaders at West Sound Treatment Center, O'Hana House, The Lighthouse, and Forward Bound programs in Kitsap County, Washington. It is an honor and a blessing to walk shoulder-to-shoulder with all of you. Your examples of overcoming personal adversity and your willingness to roll up your sleeves and do the right thing is indeed saving lives and changing the world. Together, we have and will continue to move mountains.

Thank you to the many hundreds of people I have known who have overcome their negativity and created their amazing lives despite incredible odds. Thank you for trusting me with your hearts and for sharing your stories, challenges, and successes with me over the last twenty-five years. To say that I have learned much more from you than you could ever learn from me is an understatement. As a good friend and soul sister of mine, Renate, always says, "Walk tall!"

Last, but definitely not least, to my coach and mentor Patrick Snow, thank you for your expertise and knowledge but most of all thank you for your example of achieving your own destiny and for believing in mine. To my talented team of publishing support: editor and amazing author Tyler Tichelaar, graphic design guru Shiloh Schroeder, and Aviva Publishing, thank you for helping me create my amazing life in tangible form! Thank you to Joe and all of my new author friends and family. I couldn't have broken through and embraced the huge changes in my life without your support and example.

Contents

Foreword

BY PATRICK SNOW

Growing up in Michigan as the fourth of five kids to loving parents and siblings, I was sheltered from many of the adversities that people face today: poverty, drugs, alcohol, broken families, homelessness, and hunger. We had financial challenges as a family, but we always had a roof over our heads and food on the table. With my dad working long hours as a teacher and coach, it was my mother who was the glue that kept our family together and well-nourished.

Everything changed one night when I was thirteen years old. On May 29th, 1982, a drunk driver pulled into our driveway at a terrible speed and accelerated as he hit the side of our house, crashing into our gas meter/gas line.

Immediately upon impact, the house exploded into a ball of flames and burned for an hour until the firefighters were successfully able to turn off the gas main. At the time of the impact, we were all inside, but thankfully, we made it out of the home unharmed.

After the fire was put out, we stood there in shock, not believing what had just happened. My mother gathered us all together, and she said these words: "Everything is going to be fine. We are all safely together, no one has died, and everything will be okay."

Now think about this: When she said this, she no longer had a place for her family to sleep (half of the house had burned down), she had no food to feed her five children, and of course, we had only the clothes on our backs and no place to go!

In this moment, seeing my mother control her response to this adversity (being that she couldn't control the actual event), I realized that her ability to remain positive not only comforted us all, but that her positive attitude was so powerful! It gave her the ability to rise above the situation, and above her own grief and loss, so she could be there for those she loved most.

In this incredible book by Robin O'Grady, you will learn that you are the driving force of your life, you are in control of your feelings and reactions, and you are the only one who can accept or reject change. You will learn that you too (just as my mother did) get to choose how you live your live and either focus on and dwell in the negative, or look on the bright side and create solutions to reach the positive.

In *The Optimist's Edge*, Robin O'Grady will help you learn to heal your past, forgive those who have betrayed you including yourself, embrace change, steer clear of negativity, and much, much more. You will be inspired by the numerous tools, stories, and quotes that will serve as a guiding force in your life. You will have the opportunity to identify and reflect on your thoughts, beliefs, and emotions as you complete the exercises in this book designed to allow you to create the life of your dreams.

When you follow the strategies, techniques, and ideas offered in this groundbreaking book, you will prepare the foundation for a new way of life, develop your own optimist's edge, and become a powerful and unstoppable force fully capable of living and achieving the vision of how you want your life to be. You will be the driving force that pre-determines your destiny instead of living by default and settling for mediocrity. You will gain the insights and tools you need to achieve the success that you want and deserve, and in the process, you will experience a much higher level of passion, joy, and peace of mind. You will find the freedom to become the very best version of yourself and in turn become a better leader, a better parent and partner, and a better member of your community.

So let Robin O'Grady, an amazing speaker, author, and coach, guide you through and move you past the land mines of negativity that rule and condition our world to find the happiness you seek. She will help you get from wherever you are to the place you want to be. Get ready for a new way of life and a new attitude. Buckle your seatbelt and brace yourself for an amazing journey! You may never again be the same!

Enjoy…

Patrick Snow

International Best-Selling Author of *Creating Your Own Destiny* and *The Affluent Entrepreneur*

www.PatrickSnow.com

Introduction

"Take the first step in faith. You don't have to see the whole staircase, just take the first step."

—Martin Luther King, Jr.

On August 17th, 1988, I made the single most important decision that I would ever make. I chose to live. Have you ever thought about ending your life? Have you ever felt hopeless because your life wasn't what you'd hoped it would be? Have you ever felt stuck and like everyone else had the secrets to good living and abundance but you? Have you ever felt so alone, broke, sick, or disgusted with your life that you just didn't want to wake up anymore? Have you ever wished that you could have more love, money, joy, and good health in your life, but you weren't sure where to start?

I get it. I've been there, and I've walked many miles in those shoes. I understand what it feels like to be hopeless and feel like an outsider. The good news is there's a light at the end of the tunnel. I can help you become the person you've always hoped to be and to have the amazing life you've always wanted to have.

This book is a road map that will provide you with the tools and strategies to change your thinking and behavior to create the life you have always imagined. If you've struggled with adversity and negative thinking, which have limited your ability to live the amazing life you are meant to live, then this book is for you!

I will teach you how to overcome negative thinking, move past your poverty mindset to create unlimited abundance, give you new tools and strategies to cope effectively with change, help you to let go of your past and forgive others and yourself, practice positive thinking by turning your adversity into your biggest gift, open your heart and have fulfilling relationships, and begin telling your new story so you can create your amazing new life and inspire and teach others how to do the same. You will learn how to recognize and steer clear of negativity in all of its insidious forms and to become the very best version of yourself while in the process, and invite and create more money, love, joy, and freedom into your life.

You'll gain valuable skills that will help *you* move forward to discover, create, and sustain the life you have always imagined. I will teach you a hands-on approach to help you move past your personal challenges to reconnect with you and to identify what you want and how to get it. You will discover and practice how to:

- Change your attitude and as a result change your life
- Release relationships that don't serve you
- Discontinue living in and sharing about the past to tell your NEW story, the story of how you are creating your amazing life NOW
- Transform your negative self-talk to become your own best supporter
- Turn your coal (adversity) into diamonds (assets)

- Manage your stress and learn new skills to practice self-care
- Find your passion and formulate your plan to achieve your goals
- Discover my Five Star Success System that will inspire and motivate you and align you with success

Throughout this book, you'll receive helpful, actionable strategies that you can immediately practice to begin changing your negative thinking.

Thousands of people all over the world are suffering from negative thinking. It directly contributes to bad health, bad relationships, poverty, and feelings of futility and hopelessness. It can make you feel horrible about yourself, your life, and even the world. External forces, including the media, reinforce negative thinking by promoting all of the bad news, which primarily includes drama, murder, insecurity, and personal and worldwide financial ruin.

The world needs to hear some good news! By becoming aware of your negative thinking and utilizing the simple, effective tools and strategies offered in this book, *you* can shift *your* negative thinking and begin living an optimistic, hopeful, inspired, and motivated life.

You will discover, uncover, and discard old beliefs and habits of thought that no longer serve you and begin moving forward by implementing new positive thoughts and daily actions that are proven to support positive life changes. No matter what you have experienced in your life, this book is sure to motivate, educate, and inspire you to shift your thinking and create the life you've always wanted.

There is no better time than now to begin moving toward the direction of your dreams, and because the clock keeps ticking, now is *the* time to make a commitment to change. How many times have you said, "I'll do it tomorrow" or "Maybe when I have more money or time or less stress, I will get to it," and then what happens? Time keeps flying by and we find ourselves doing the same thing over and over, settling into "just getting by," or worse, giving up on our dreams altogether.

"Sometimes the brightest light comes from the darkest place."
—Author Unknown

But what makes me the expert anyway? On August 17th, 1988, I had an epiphany that would indeed begin to change my thinking and propel me forward into seeking and yes, creating, the amazing life I had only before dreamt could be true for me. I'll never forget that day because in hindsight, I don't know that I ever really thrived before that moment. I'd been barely surviving and living my life, in essence, by default. I was spiritually, emotionally, and physically bankrupt and had no idea how to better my life or even where to start.

Like so many other people, I experienced multiple barriers in my early life, and I suppose my story is worse than some but not as bad as others. I grew up with poverty, domestic violence, and drug abuse. I went to fourteen different schools because we moved so much and I was never quite sure what was going to happen next. Some days when I would walk into the house after school, everyone would be happy and there was a celebratory vibe. Other days when I would walk into the house, it was like walking straight into hell.

I was confused, sad, and scared most of the time, and I began to wonder why I was born in the first place. I took my first drink of alcohol when I was nine years old, and by the time I was thirteen, I was using alcohol and other drugs regularly to cope with my negative feelings. I perpetuated my own self-created hell on earth, and I believed that because of the challenges I had grown up with, I was permanently crippled, broken, and undeserving of anything or anyone worthwhile in my life.

Through my own negative thinking and behaviors, I created an environment that supported my beliefs, often putting myself in harm's way and in some very dark, scary places, and I believed that was where I belonged, but on August 17th, 1988, I was given a second chance at life.

I was lying on the floor of my dingy apartment that night, crying and praying to some*one*, some*thing*, just to end my life. I didn't have enough courage to commit suicide, but I could not stand the thought of waking up for one more day. If the life I was living were all there was for me, I didn't want it anymore. I cried out to God, the dark, someone, whoever would hear my appeal, "Please take my life or help me!" This was my dark night of the soul, the catalyst for change that I had heard other people describe when they were at the very ends of their ropes.

The chain of events that occurred next was nothing short of miraculous. I had a moment of clarity that I can only describe as God-given insight or divine intervention. I got up off the floor, and it felt as if I were literally being pushed into action, animated by something much stronger than myself. I believe now that I was filled with the Holy Spirit, and though I am not a religious person, I believe from my head to my toes that God stepped in and plucked me straight from the depths of hell and delivered me somewhere safe in that moment. I got dressed and called my brother, who came immediately and picked me up to take me to the hospital's detoxification unit. I had been trapped in a cycle of negative thinking, emotional torment, and addiction for eleven long, hopeless years. After checking in at the hospital, I sat utterly defeated on the edge of my detox bed. I was relieved and horrified all at once.

In that moment, I was filled with the awareness that everything I had ever known was about to change forever. I thought about the wreckage that I'd created because of my years of drug and alcohol abuse, the people I had lied to and hurt, and all the time I had wasted, and as I crawled into the detox bed, my last thoughts were "Thank God it's finally over; I don't have to fight anymore." Despite my bewilderment and horror that day, I surrendered to the unknown with full intention. That was twenty-five years ago, and I have *never* looked back.

So you see, just like thousands of people all over the world, there was a time when I was struggling to find meaning and joy in my life and trying to figure out how to improve my circumstances, but I was painfully focused on and stuck in my life's negative aspects. I had dug a hole with my negative thinking, and it wasn't until I hit an emotional wall that I realized it was time to reevaluate the tools in my toolbox and replace them with new tools that would help me create the life I *really* wanted to live.

"Unless you puke, faint or die, keep going."
—Jillian Michaels

I'd love to tell you that my journey was an easy one from then on, but that was not the case. Getting sober was only the very beginning, and I'd built up years of garbage that needed to be resolved. Painful and repetitive thoughts about the trauma I experienced in my childhood, my own history of bad relationships, and the shame, guilt, and self-loathing from my years of selfishness were all constant negative companions in my head, and believe me, they weren't good company. Like a non-stop committee of critics, the voices in my head choked-out any chance of experiencing feelings of happiness and contentment.

While my life had improved considerably because I wasn't drinking and using drugs anymore, I still felt an emptiness inside that nothing seemed to quell. It felt like I had a hole in my soul, and no matter how much money, food, sex, attention, or recognition I received, I still felt something big was missing. It was as if my very spirit were hungry. While I wanted change with all my might, I lacked the skills I needed to move beyond the negativity to create the life I knew I was destined for—a life of hope, success, purpose, and joy.

From the beginning of what I consider my second chance in life, I have worked diligently to replace my old coping tools and strategies, which weren't working for me anymore, with new effective tools and strategies. The discovery and practice of these simple and amazing tools and strategies has helped me experience joy, a life of purpose and meaning, and I have had more success than I could have ever imagined. The tools in this book helped me cope in the hardest of times with painful life events like divorce, the death of loved ones, and other major life changes. They have improved my relationships and provided me with more joy, love, money, good health, and self-worth than I ever thought possible. I'm no longer a hostage in my own life, and I'm often asked why I'm always so happy by my peers, coworkers, and friends.

Over a span of twenty-four years in my professional career as a leader, counselor, author, speaker, and coach, I've shared these same tools and strategies with hundreds of people who report that they've been able to move beyond *their own* negativity to create amazing, successful, and fulfilling lives.

Growing up while attending the school of hard knocks wasn't easy, but it has been invaluable because it has motivated, inspired, and propelled me to do better and be better. When I was twenty-five, I was able to go back to college and get my counseling degree. Over the last twenty-plus years, I have made it my mission to educate, inspire, and motivate as many people as I can while creating my own amazing life and leaving an inspiring legacy for my community and my family.

My life is incredible today. I have a wonderful husband, two amazing teenage boys who never fail to surprise and delight me, and a great professional career, in which I get to help people create their amazing lives every day. But most importantly, I have the knowing that I am responsible and accountable for creating the outcomes of my own life. I call the shots; I decide what experiences I want to have. I get to have, be, and do anything of my choosing!

Even if you're functioning well and are experiencing a satisfying level of success in your life, you may not feel you're doing your best or that you're functioning at your optimum level. Many people have told me that although they've had a decent quality of life and fulfilling relationships, they also have an emptiness inside that they can't seem to fill. Still others say they aren't particularly connected with their work, or they have a deeper calling that they've never honored or followed through with.

I understand your apprehension about making changes in your life. You have every right to be apprehensive. It's okay. I understand. I was afraid too, mostly because I feared change and the possibility that I would fail, but I am here to help you. I want to be your coach and mentor and help you move past your unique and personal challenges to create your amazing life, the life you were born to live. I will walk shoulder-to-shoulder with you as your advisor and your friend. We can walk this journey together!

This book is your missing link and *my* calling. It is the physical manifestation, the tangible evidence that I have moved beyond my own negative thinking and behavior. My amazing life began when I started changing my negative thinking and began sharing the valuable tools and strategies I have discovered and practiced with the world. With each new day, I'm creating the life of my dreams, and now, it's your turn. This book will help shorten your learning curve and help you create the life of your dreams. Let me guide you through the process of overcoming your negativity and turning your adversity into your biggest asset. I challenge you now to move beyond negative thinking to create *your* amazing life. Are you ready? Good! Your journey begins today, so let's go!

Chapter 1

Understanding Negative Thinking

"Negative thoughts stick around because we believe them, not because we want them or choose them."

—Andrew Bernstein

Do you spend a lot of time thinking negative thoughts or focusing on the negative things about your life? Have you ever become aware that you are focused on the negative and tried to begin thinking positively only to find that very quickly you were focused on the negative again? Did you know that negative thinking is caused by habitual thinking patterns connected to your core beliefs about yourself, your relationships, money, security, and life in general?

I had a coworker years ago who was a total "negative Nelly!" It didn't matter what we were talking about; she would put a negative spin on the conversation. Even at times when I would purposely try to shift our conversation to something positive, she would promptly return it to something negative. Why would she do this?

Your core beliefs are a filter through which you see yourself and the world around you, and they dictate your behavior sometimes without you even realizing it. For instance, if you believe you can't make a good living because you are not very smart, and therefore, you only apply for jobs that pay minimum wage, you are, in effect reinforcing your belief that you can't make a good living. Another example is if you believe that you are unworthy of love, you will repeatedly participate in relationships in which you don't feel loved, thereby proving to yourself that you aren't worthy of love.

YOU ARE SMARTER THAN YOU KNOW

"The measure of intelligence is the ability to change."
—Albert Einstein

When I finally went back to college to get my general education at age twenty-five, I was newly sober, and I'm pretty sure I was still a couple of bricks shy of a full-load. I struggled with a short attention span, but more than that, I had the fundamental core belief that I wasn't very smart. As I continued on in school, I kept getting A's and B's in my college classes, but my response to that was "Gee, these classes must be really easy or something!" I remember realizing one day, after receiving an A on a very difficult history project I had submitted, that it wasn't that the class was easy, but rather, "I am pretty darn smart!" I can't tell you how exciting it was for me finally to discover the truth—that I am indeed and in fact always have been really smart—and to uncover and discard this negative core belief that had contributed to my low self-worth and had limited my options in life for so long! Acknowledging my own intelligence was the defining brick in the foundation that became my *new* life.

EXERCISE:

What negative core beliefs do you have that no longer serve whom you want to become?

How have these core beliefs affected your self-worth?

How have these core beliefs affected your relationships with others?

How have these core beliefs affected your finances?

How have these core beliefs affected your security and the way you see the world?

___

___

___

___

___

But your negative thinking doesn't just affect you, does it? No, it also affects the people around you, including your loved ones, your coworkers, and even strangers who cross your path over the course of the day. When you are constantly negative, miserable, and complaining, or counting on your loved ones to define your happiness, or when you blame someone else for your misery or you focus on their shortcomings to distract you from your own, you actually repel people from you. No one likes to be around someone who is constantly negative, miserable, or irritable.

I once had a married couple for neighbors, and the husband had some pretty serious health problems. He talked about his health problems all the time, and I do mean all the time. It was as if he literally had nothing else to talk about. His wife, trying to be a good wife I'm sure, fed this constant negative discussion about her husband's poor health by also making it the focus of conversations with her husband, friends, neighbors, and family. Eventually, she began to experience depression and sleeping problems, and she often remarked that she was fearful and had anxiety about her future as a result of her husband's bad health. This couple did not realize it at the time, but they were making his health problems worse by constantly focusing on them, and not only that, she was beginning to get sick too! Whatever you focus on expands, and your health is no exception. Obviously, he had some issues that needed to be discussed, but focusing primarily on the negative brings more negative.

When people are negative, they are often hoping somehow to alleviate their own concerns about something and receive concern, attention, commiseration, and sympathy from others. Receiving this attention is the pay off for being negative, but the very action of your negativity actually repels a person away from you, resulting in the opposite of what it is you're trying to accomplish in the first place. Some people are even aware of this fact, so why then do they continue being so negative?

STUCK IN A RUT

"There is little difference in people, but that little difference makes a big difference. That little difference is attitude. The big difference is whether it is positive or negative."
—Robert Collier

I had a friend who was a gentle soul, but she was so negative that I felt like she sucked my spirit right out of me every time we talked. She called me on the phone almost every day, and she would immediately begin talking about all of the horrible things that were happening in her life—her inattentive husband, her lack of money, and her horrible physical problems. She would keep me on the phone for an hour telling me about how terrible everything was in her life. Sooner than later, I didn't want to pick up the phone when I knew it was her calling. When I saw her in the market, I was literally repelled and felt like hiding completely or going in the opposite direction.

Despite my discomfort, I really wanted to be a good friend to her. I hoped I might be able to help her and brighten her day in some way. I tried to be of service to her, to help her find solutions to her problems, and sometimes, I just gave her a listening ear. Eventually though, I felt as if I were being used, and it became obvious that she had no intention of doing anything about her problems. She was stuck in a rut of cyclical (and toxic) negative thinking. The more she talked and thought about negative people, places, and things, the more negativity she attracted into her life. She was creating her own hell like I had done for so long earlier in my life, so I knew I needed to remove myself from the relationship.

Because I didn't want to be rude and I wasn't quite sure how to end the relationship, I allowed it to go on longer than I really wanted, but once I ended the relationship, she very quickly found another friend who lived on her block with whom she had more in common, and they became instant friends. I still felt a little guilty about ending the relationship, but I felt just as compelled to break it off because my busy family and work schedule doesn't leave me much time to socialize, and I have a deep need for meaningful friendships based on mutual support and positivity.

Interestingly, a payoff *always* exists for staying in a toxic relationship. It may be that you need to feel needed or that you're gaining some other payoff by participating in the relationship.

It's okay to end relationships with people who are toxic for you. In fact, with practice, you can avoid and not get involved in toxic relationships before they start. Although this may be a new concept, it is important to begin setting healthy boundaries and honoring your own value and self-worth in relationships. Soon with your new improved positive attitude, you'll find yourself surrounded by supportive positive people, often without much effort on your part.

EXERCISE:

Ask yourself some questions:

What is it that you need from your friendships?

____

____

____

____

____

What is it that you have to offer to your friendships?

____

____

____

____

____

Are you participating in any friendships that don't serve you or that are not based on equal reciprocal ground?

____

____

____

____

____

If so, what is the payoff for you to stay in these relationships?

____

____

____

____

____

People stay stuck in the rut of negative thinking for many reasons, but one thing is for sure, remaining stagnant can compound negative feelings, depression, and low self-worth, and it affirms the core belief that you aren't worth the effort to change. The only difference between stagnancy and the life of your dreams is action. Be willing and ready to take action, especially when it means leaving negative people, places, and things behind so you can have more room for positive people, places, and things.

The definition of mediocrity is *ordinary and not exceptional in any way*. In reality, you are anything but mediocre because we are *all* extraordinary, unique, and exceptional in our *own* ways. Extraordinary means that we are *exceptional, beyond what is usual* and this is what we, each of us, really are. Deep inside, you know you are exceptional and meant to live an amazing life, but when you don't honor and act on this reality, you become conflicted, depressed, and confused about who you are and what you want to do in your life. That is when you find yourself settling for less than what you really deserve in life, love, work, and in your health. Sometimes it can feel easier just to get by day-to-day than to face the fear of the unknown and take the positive action necessary to move forward and create change.

When you are in the habit of being negative, just the very repetition of doing something over and over can create a false feeling of safety and security. Knowing what to expect even if it's negative can be comforting somehow, especially when it's all you've known. Some other reasons why you may find yourself stuck in the rut of negative thinking include:

- **Fear of Change:** Good or bad change can be scary and throw you off balance. For instance, getting a new great job is a wonderful thing, but it can also bring up many thoughts such as "Am I going to be able to do a good job?" and can also bring up feelings of fear and insecurity. Losing a job is another example that could potentially bring up negative thoughts such as "Am I not good enough?" "Was it something I did/didn't do?" and feelings of inadequacy and depression.
- **Fear of Stepping Out of Your Comfort Zone:** Being afraid to step out of your comfort zone is another example of why someone may choose to stay in a rut. Your comfort zone feels safe and you know what to expect so you have the feeling that you are in control. Stepping out of your comfort zone can be risky and cause feelings of anxiety, fear, and of being out of control.
- **Low Self-Worth:** Feeling that you don't deserve a good life or that you won't succeed if you try can hinder your willingness to do new things and keep you stuck in a rut.

- **Internalizing the Opinions and Feelings of Others:** While being compassionate and caring means considering other people's feelings and opinions, when you abandon your *own* feelings and opinions to please others, you are not being compassionate and caring toward yourself. It's important to honor and express your feelings and opinions regardless of whether other people agree or validate them. Your opinions and feelings are as valid and important as the opinions and feelings of others.
- **Procrastination:** Not taking action is a sure way to stay stuck in a rut. Why wait until tomorrow to do what you can do today? Taking action now leaves tomorrow open for something even *more* amazing!
- **Not Knowing Where to Start:** Looking at the whole picture can be overwhelming and can create the feeling of being immobilized. Instead, you can break your tasks down to simple daily actions that are manageable. Not only will you begin getting stuff done, but you will feel accomplished in the process!
- **Fear of Failure:** The fear of failure can be scary. Taking action involves taking risks and taking risks can feel really uncomfortable. The way you feel about yourself is an indicator of how successful you will become. If you can see it, you can be it! Truth be told, many people are actually as afraid of success as they are of failure. Which is scarier? The fear of failure or the fear of success?

EXERCISE:

Pick the top three indicators listed above that you have personally experienced. How have these indicators kept you stuck in a rut?

1. ____

____

2. ____

____

3. ____

____

DON'T BE A SCHLEPROCK

"I just need somewhere to dump all my negativity."
—Van Morrison

When I was little, I used to watch an old cartoon by Hanna-Barbera called *The Pebbles & Bamm-Bamm Show*. In it was a character named Schleprock. Everyone hated it when Schleprock came around because as soon as he stepped into the room, everything went to hell in a handbasket. Literally, the roof would cave in and everything would start crumbling at his presence. His favorite catch phrase was, "Oh wowsie wowsie woo woo. Miserable day, isn't it?" Do you know someone like this?

I had an acquaintance whom I would see from time to time at the local hardware store or produce market in my town, and when I would ask her how she was, she would begin to tell me the deepest and darkest details of why her life was so miserable. As soon as she began talking, my eyes would glaze over and I would literally have the urge to run away screaming.

My acquaintance was so focused on negativity so much of the time that she became a beacon of negativity—a virtual vortex of negative energy followed her and emanated from her like a cloud everywhere she went. Don't be a Schleprock! Don't dump your negativity on others. When you become aware that you are dumping it on others, quit.

I believe that in general people care about each other, but I also learned from this person that there is a time and a place to self-disclose your innermost life. When people in a public setting ask you how you are, they don't really want to know the details! The expectation is that you will respond briefly and superficially. Now, if you are with a close friend having coffee or in another intimate social setting, it would be appropriate to disclose more about your personal life, but even then, hopefully you will keep the negativity to a minimum.

NEGATIVE THINKING = NEGATIVE FEELINGS

"Bondage is subjection to external influences and internal negative thoughts and attitudes."
—W. Clement Stone

Negative thinking can become a crippling debilitating habit and can create a myriad of negative feelings including depression, anger, and anxiety. It can isolate you from the people you love the most, causing even further negative feelings. It can affect your physical health by creating stress in your body. Negative thinking is emotionally painful, can make you feel trapped in your own life, and can cause feelings of hopelessness and futility. It can even lead to suicidal ideation or suicide attempts in their worst form.

My dear friend Sandy had a serious mental health condition, and as a result, she took several medications, many of which caused side effects such as difficulty managing her emotions, persistent depression, and tardive dyskinesia (a mostly irreversible neurological disorder of involuntary movements caused by long-term use of antipsychotic or neuroleptic drugs) to name a few. She struggled so much with negative thinking that she hated her own guts. According to her self-report, her entire chain of thought consisted of how she was not good enough, no one liked her, she was ugly and fat, and she believed herself to be crazy, but that was not how I and many of our mutual friends perceived her; Sandy was one of the most loving and generous people we knew. She loved animals and children, and she would do anything to help someone in need. She was the first to take in stray animals (and sometimes people). She often shared her slender resources and food with those who needed them most, but best of all, she had an amazing and hilarious sense of humor, despite her many challenges. She was loved, and she inspired everyone who crossed her path with her loving spirit and kindness.

Sandy died when she was thirty-six years old. Her mental illness was stabilized at the time of her death, but many people in our community believe she died due to the wear and tear of years of taking multiple medications. When she died, she was surrounded by people who loved her. Why Sandy was unable to identify and build on her positive qualities could be attributed to her mental illness or the many medications she took, but how she felt about herself and her ongoing chain of negative thinking are not so uncommon even among people without mental illnesses. Over the years, Sandy and many others I have known have shared several common recurring negative thoughts:

- I never have enough (money, time, love, attention...)
- I'm too (old, young, dumb, fat, broke…)
- I am damaged or incomplete because of the things that have happened to me in my past
- People always take advantage of me; I am a victim
- If he/she would just___________, then I would be happy
- I am not a good (wife, husband, parent, friend)
- I am not strong or worthy enough
- If people knew who I really am, they wouldn't love me
- My feelings, opinions, and dreams are not important
- No one *really* appreciates, loves, or cares about me

These common and repetitive negative thoughts can become like a broken record in your head if allowed to continue. Let's see how they affect you in the following exercise:

EXERCISE:

Do you identify with any of the above negative thoughts? If so, which ones?

____

____

____

____

____

What other negative thoughts are you aware of that cause you to experience negative feelings?

____

____

____

____

____

How have these negative feelings about yourself affected your relationships with others?

____

____

____

____

____

How have these negative feelings affected your physical, emotional, and spiritual health?

____

____

____

____

____

What are five new positive thoughts you can repeat to yourself when you become aware that you are listening to *your* broken record of negativity?

____

____

____

____

____

Who in his or her right mind ever dreamt of one day growing up to be negative and cynical? Negative thinking is something that happens over time, sometimes even subconsciously, and it affects and infects our mental, physical, and spiritual health and wellness and our closest relationships. You can change your negative thinking by practicing the new tools and strategies you will read about in this book. You can become free from the limiting and painful feelings and beliefs that drive your negative thinking and behaviors, and you can create the life you have always imagined. You are the master of your own destiny and your thinking can be your best friend or worst enemy.

Love, joy, and fulfillment are always available to you. They are your God-given natural blessings, but they are only possible when *you* believe in *yourself*! Believing in yourself means acknowledging your unique attributes and having faith that you can do anything you put your mind to. Believing in yourself means taking action even if you can't yet see the positive outcomes. This self-trust is conscious, joyful, inspired living, and once you begin the forward momentum, you become unstoppable!

YOUR BELIEFS DICTATE YOUR BEHAVIOR

"Everything that happens to you is a reflection of what you believe about yourself. We cannot outperform our level of self-esteem. We cannot draw to ourselves more than we think we are worth."

—Iyanla Vanzant

Because of the adversity and the dysfunctional environment I experienced growing up, some personal dynamics naturally occurred for me. Some of these dynamics included: I wasn't allowed to talk about what was really going on because the truth would hurt others too much, it was scary, or it threatened those around me because it meant something might have to change; I wasn't allowed to have feelings or opinions about what was happening around me; and I was expected somehow just to "get over" my responses to what was happening around me and to me. Because I was small and didn't have the wherewithal to fend for myself, I was completely powerless over my life and the ability to protect myself. I couldn't trust my environment because it wasn't safe and had no consistency or routine.

In this unstable, sometimes volatile environment, I developed many mistaken beliefs, including: I am responsible for the feelings of others, but I'm not allowed to have any of my own; the needs of other people come before my own, and it is selfish of me to want or expect anything; and I am powerless over the events that happen in my life. As a result of these mistaken beliefs, I wasted years and cried many tears because I didn't believe I mattered or really deserved anything good.

At one point when I was asked about myself, I jokingly would say, "I am no one from nowhere." That response was a direct reflection of how I felt on the inside. Remembering that now brings tears to my eyes because today I know what a valuable and precious human being I am and how much I have to give to the world, but it wasn't until I could really examine my beliefs, lay them out on the table, and shine the light of reason on them, that I could begin to believe in myself.

Your belief system's construction begins when you are very small through modeling the behavior, values, and morals of your caretakers and environment. This modeling shapes the beliefs you have about yourself, others, and the world. These beliefs can be found at your very core, and though they may mutate and change as you gain new life experiences, your beliefs control your feelings and your choices, and they may or may not be based on reality or present circumstances.

For example, if you grew up poor or in an environment that was emotionally, physically, or verbally abusive, you may have the core belief that you deserve to be abused. Until this belief is identified for what it is (an old belief that is based in untruth), and new tools for change are implemented, it can affect your self-worth, your ability to be close with others, and the choices you make about your relationships and personal economic stability.

A couple I knew, Rick and Robin, couldn't seem to live with or without each other. They treated each other horribly, verbally (and sometimes even physically) assaulting each other in front of their friends and families and constantly breaking up and making up. Although many other dynamics were involved that affected their relationship in derogatory ways, the bottom line was that both of them had been raised in environments that included physical and verbal abuse by their parents. Because they were never taught that this behavior was unacceptable or given the skills to have healthy, fulfilling relationships, they had no clue how to behave any differently. Both were miserable and took their misery out on each other and everyone else. Eventually, Rick ended up in jail for domestic violence and Robin ended up with a substance abuse disorder.

Robin was able to get help via a treatment program and Rick later agreed to attend a domestic violence perpetrator program. However, they were unable to repair their relationship and later separated. Because they carried their childhood belief systems into their adult lives, they suffered and had ineffective and hurtful relationships. Can you see how their early belief systems modeled and dictated their adult lives? Until you are able to unlearn the toxic beliefs and replace them with new and positive beliefs, you are unlikely to change.

On the opposite spectrum, if you grew up in a system where family members were respected and nurtured, you more likely would have the core belief that *you* deserve to be nurtured and treated with respect. It would also follow that you would nurture others and treat them respectfully as well.

EXERCISE:

What were some of the behaviors modeled by your caretakers while you were growing up?

____

____

____

____

____

What were some of the messages you received that became your beliefs as a result of this modeled behavior?

____

____

____

____

____

Which of these beliefs do not serve you in your adult life? What do you need to change in order to be who it is you want to be and deserve to be?

What were some values and morals that were modeled by your caretakers?

Of the values and morals modeled by your caretakers, which ones do you want to keep and which ones do you want to get rid of?

SUMMARY

Every one of your core beliefs has a story to support and back it up. Your story is your personal perception and accounting of how you got to where you are today. If your story is negative and has caused you considerable heartache, at some point you have to make a conscious decision to change your story in an effort to forge ahead. The truth is that you are the one who holds the key to your own success and it begins with examining and changing your beliefs. You will need to accept doing that work if you are ready to make positive changes.

Your contentment is an inside job. No person, place, or thing has the power to stand in the way of your happiness, your joy, and the life you desire. When you become accountable for and take ownership of your own life, you'll begin the process of moving forward and quickly!

Chapter 2

Overcoming Negativity

"You must not allow yourself to dwell for a single moment on any kind of negative thought."
—Emmet Fox

EXTERNAL NEGATIVITY

In the first chapter, we discussed how and why we become negative thinkers and how negative thinking directly creates negative behaviors and can cause you to make negative choices. Your underlying belief system was created early on from what you saw modeled in your environment, and it can actually dictate your behavior as an adult in the present. But negativity also can creep into your life in other ways to take away from your serenity.

Have you ever really noticed the negativity coming at you from external sources? Have you ever found yourself slipping into negativity when you spend time in a negative environment or with negative people or watching negative stuff on TV?

Being bombarded by external negativity is the number one offender to your peace of mind. External negativity includes negativity as experienced, read, and heard in the media such as newspapers, magazines, television, and movies, and it is also a direct result of being subjected to other people's negativity. But let's start with the media....

One afternoon, I decided to do an experiment and went to our local cable TV channel guide to see what was on. On this particular day, the programming included: *Trauma: Life in the ER*, *1,000 Ways to Die*, *When Animals Attack*, *When Girls Kill*, *Snapped*, *Fatal Attraction*, *Let's Go To Prison*, and *Greed*. Yes, seriously. No offense meant, but you have to ask yourself whether watching these programs is how you want to spend your time. Will watching these shows contribute to your wellbeing and support a positive attitude?

When my children were little, I paid full attention to the media they were exposed to, but I didn't think much about its affect on me personally. I was shocked and concerned when I realized what the TV show options were for my kids! Becoming mindful of what my children were watching made me also consider the effects of what I was watching.

When you spend time watching or listening to negativity, it affects your mood and feelings. The same holds true for positivity, so if you choose to watch TV, make sure it is something that will support your new way of thinking.

For instance, if you love to travel, try watching *House Hunters International* or the Travel Channel, which will expose you to interesting places and teach you about different cultures. Limiting not only the time you spend watching TV, but what you're actually watching can have a significant effect on your overall wellbeing.

Do yourself a favor—turn off the TV and use the time you would spend watching TV to create your amazing life instead!

Read a great book, listen to personal development CDs or audio books, learn about someone you admire, take a class online or at your local college, walk, or meditate. Positive actions equal positive consequences. Check out goodnewsnetwork.org, which provides a "daily dose of compelling good news."

The media also uses magazines, newspapers, and radio to spread the news of worldwide fear, trauma, negativity, and gossip. Next time you're in the grocery store's checkout line, take a good look around. The magazine stands are filled with gossip about celebrity break-ups and how much weight celebrities have gained or lost, their alleged affairs, the soon to come "end of the world," and many other negative messages. I am not suggesting that you shut yourself off from the world, but I am suggesting that you consider how you can minimize the negative influence of these forms of media and what you choose to put into your head and heart.

Keeping negativity at its right size can be challenging, but the more you practice, the better you'll become at making choices that support your positive attitude.

EXERCISE:

What effect has the media (TV, radio, newspapers, magazines, etc.) had on your ability to be positive?

____

____

____

____

____

What are you willing to do to minimize the negativity you experience from the media?

____

____

____

____

____

Personally, I no longer watch the news, although I do catch snippets of it because my husband watches it in the evening. I also peruse the newspaper headlines in the market or at the gas station when getting gas. For the most part, I overhear world event conversations on a continual basis from those at work or friends, but I rarely sit down and actually watch the entire newscast. I don't miss it one bit, and I have better ways to spend my time than catastrophizing over redundant negative news and the traumatic event of the day or week.

NEGATIVITY AND YOUR LOVED ONES

"Live and Let Live."
—Mahatma Gandhi

Now let's take a look at negative people. But first, you might wonder what to do if the negativity in your life is coming from the people you love most such as your children, spouse, or a parent? Do you have tools available to "not take-on" the negativity of your loved ones, or do you tend to internalize and feel responsible for changing or fixing the negativity of others?

I've found it best to stay on my own side of the street in such matters and just let others be who they are. Rather than try to change them (and by the way, you can't change anyone else), I work on myself and my perception of them. I find that this change of focus attracts those I love toward me, rather than repels them away from me. When I can be tolerant and understanding toward others and put the shoe on the other foot, I feel better and don't get hooked into their negativity. Not everyone is ready to change like you. Let them be. Hopefully at some point, they may want what you have inside for themselves, and then you can tell them what you've done to change. In the meantime, live and let live.

On a more challenging scale, if you have the tendency to suffer from taking on the negativity of your loved ones, you may be "getting hooked." Getting hooked is what happens when you internalize someone else's concerns, feelings, or bad attitude and allow that negativity to rub off on you. I liken this to someone handing you a jacket to wear that doesn't belong to you, but you put it on anyway in an effort to be caring and polite. The jacket isn't your style at all, it's hot and uncomfortable, and it stinks really bad, but you wear it nonetheless because you feel you're obligated to do so, but you're not.

You have a choice, and you have the power to take off the jacket and give it back to the person who gave it to you. You don't have to be mean or callous about it; just give it back and wish the best for the person. This response can be very difficult and can take practice, but you can become very good at it. Not getting hooked doesn't mean that you don't care or that you're indifferent; it just means that you acknowledge that you're responsible for yourself and others are responsible for themselves, and you care enough about yourself not to get involved in what is none of your business to begin with.

For example, your mate is in a horrible mood and begins to take it out on you by being short with you. He goes on a five-minute rant about why things aren't happening the way he thinks they should, and then he asks why you don't see it his way? Rather than turn it into a fight or take it personally, you can be aware that it is just what it is. Your mate is in a bad mood, and it has nothing to do with you. Remove yourself from the situation, carry on with your business, and don't put on the jacket. Make a decision to let it go, and don't lose sleep over it or turn it into a bigger than life drama. Letting it go will help you stay positive when others aren't.

YOU ARE NOT A REFLECTION OF OTHERS

> "Every human has four endowments—self-awareness,
> conscience, independent will and creative imagination.
> These give us the ultimate human freedom...
> The power to choose, to respond, to change."
> **—Stephen Covey**

Have you ever blamed yourself for someone else's bad behavior, thinking there must have been something you said or did to cause it or something you could have done to prevent it? "If I were just a better _______ (friend, lover, wife, employee), or if I would have, I should have, I could have, then maybe…." *When people treat you badly, act in selfish ways, or make hurtful choices, their behavior does not define you—it defines them.*

As you begin to become comfortable in your own skin, you will experience an intuitive knowing inside of you that someone else's bad behavior is not only *not* about you, but you even get to the place where you can detach from others with love. Detaching doesn't mean you don't care about them—it means you care enough about yourself not to get hooked into their toxic drama. You learn that you are responsible for your own choices and how you respond to others. Here are some helpful hints you can use to steer clear from negativity that does not belong to you:

- Remove yourself physically from the situation and get busy. Don't take it on or give it any energy. Remember, it's not about you.
- Write about it. Keep a journal and you will be amazed by what you find out about yourself. Usually when I begin writing about something specific, I find out there is much more going on inside of me below the surface. A wise friend told me once that *there is something that happens between the heart and the pen that does not occur between the mind and the mouth.*
- Pray for that person, whether you mean it or not. Bless him and wish for him all the things you wish for yourself. Eventually, you will find through repetition that you no longer harbor resentment for the person as a result.

Do what you can to forgive and do it for *yourself.* It takes a toll on the mind, body, and soul to stay angry and carry resentment. Do not underestimate the benefits to you of forgiving others. No one is perfect; we are human, which means we are all fallible. Be kind to yourself and make the decision to "drop the rock" and let it go. If a situation is unacceptable to you or not in alignment with your values and morals, do yourself a favor and move on. If someone treats you badly consistently and you allow it to continue, you're giving that person permission to treat you badly, and while you are not responsible for that person's behavior, *you are responsible for your own behavior.*

It's okay to stay separate from others and still love them. Having a solid sense of self means you acknowledge that you have your own opinions and feelings and so do others, and that you're separate and autonomous from them. At the same time, you will find that not getting hooked will contribute greatly to your own wellbeing and positivity. When you take back your power and you choose not to let others define your happiness, you'll be amazed by how free and empowered you feel!

Here are some more ideas to help you when you feel you're being pelted with negativity. If someone else's negativity is being directed specifically toward you, you can:

- **Politely change the subject:** If someone is speaking to you about gloom and doom, you can redirect the conversation by talking about some related subject in a positive light.
- **End the conversation:** You have a right to end conversations that are negative and make you feel uncomfortable. Some quick responses to negative conversations may include: stating you forgot that you have something pressing to take care of that needs your immediate attention and remove yourself from the situation, or stating you have a prior engagement and need to get going right away. You are not obligated to participate in negative conversations ever!

- **Reply with a minimal response:** Stating "Uh-huh" or "Ah" without any further response indicates that you've heard what someone is saying while not actively involving yourself in the negativity. This response will also give you a moment to consider other ways out of the conversation.
- **Tell it like it is:** You can respond by simply and kindly stating that you're really trying to see things on the bright side these days and begin talking about something positive instead.

When it comes to people we're close to like our loved ones, if they know us well and know that we've struggled with negative thinking, being honest and forthright about our personal goal to move past our negative thinking will be well-received. If not, remember that it's still an inside job and that your wellbeing doesn't hinge on others' opinions and behaviors. Take personal responsibility for *you*, and for *your* feelings and actions, and let others do the same. You don't need anyone's approval to change, grow, and become your best!

While there's no way humanly possible to shield yourself completely from external negativity, you can limit the external negativity to which you expose yourself. Finding opportunities to experience positivity is a great way conversely to remove yourself from it. The more you focus on being positive, the more you will look for positive experiences and notice the positive in situations, and the more it'll become second nature for you to look on the bright side despite others' negativity.

EXERCISE:

What are some of the ways you've been affected by your loved ones' negativity?

____

____

____

____

____

How do you feel inside when you get hooked by other people's negativity?

____

____

____

____

____

How will you respond differently when you find yourself getting hooked by your loved ones' negativity?

____

____

____

____

____

Using some of the prior suggestions for not taking on others' negativity, what are some specific activities you can do when you find yourself getting sucked into the negativity?

____

____

____

____

____

Learn to be less sensitive to the negativity of others. You will need to toughen up and understand that others are not going to change just because you have made the choice to change, and they may not support you changing either. Some people are threatened by change and may be fearful that the changes you are making in your life will affect them, and the truth is, they are probably right. The changes you are making will affect those around you, but if they begin to see the changes are positive, they will hopefully be more likely to support you as time goes on. Either way, you need to be prepared to seek out like-minded people who will support you.

> "Self-worth comes from one thing—
> thinking that you are worthy."
> **—Wayne Dyer**

INTERNAL NEGATIVITY

In the prior section, we discussed external negativity, but what about the negativity that stems from you, your thoughts, and your own actions? Many people subconsciously sabotage their own success and squash any hope of reaching their goals and dreams by thinking and doing things that make them feel oppressed, depressed, and even hopeless, perhaps without even consciously realizing it. Some examples include:

- Belittling yourself by participating in self-deprecating jokes, stories, or conversations, and/or using self-deprecating language/cutting yourself down verbally or in your head
- Denying or minimizing your talents, desires, or potential
- Trying to "fit-in" by participating in behavior you do not agree with
- Playing it safe by dreaming small when you have bigger dreams inside
- Stifling your creativity and passion by doing what you think others want you to do rather than following your own calling and passion

Have you limited your own success? Have you minimized your talent and played it safe living day-to-day by default because it was easier, less risky, or too scary to change your life?

Do yourself a favor and stop doing these things. As covert as they may seem, they affect you, and when other people see and hear you doing these things, you negate your own value and the way others perceive you whether you realize it or not. These are all insidious ways not to be accountable for your own life. When you cut yourself down, don't make your values and morals clear, minimize your talent, or limit yourself in order to people please, you sell yourself short on so many levels.

EXERCISE:

In what ways do you cut yourself down or belittle yourself internally?

How do you belittle yourself publically?

Have you done things on the outside that don't fit who you are on the inside? What were they and why do you suppose you made those choices?

What examples can you give of times you chose to play it safe due to fear or some other concern?

Have you complied with the wishes of others and in return given up your creativity and passion as a result?

____

____

____

____

____

What are you willing to do differently? How can you provide yourself with the confidence and support you need now as you travel down a different road? A better road? The road to your dreams? How will you handle success? Will you cower down and not be accountable for it, or will you rise with it, embrace it, build on it, and become stronger because of it? Will you be the owner and leader of your new life, or will you choose to stay small and let it fade away?

Many of us, including me, have been taught that acknowledging or talking about our own positive attributes is conceited. Well, here is a new way to look at it. Who, if not you, will make sure that you reach your goals to live *and maintain* the life of your dreams? If you plan on achieving what it is you want, you are going to have to step up and learn to market yourself. You will need to be your own best cheerleader.

Admitting the *positive* things about you is a way of practicing humility. Smart and successful people take an accurate stock of themselves—both the good *and* the bad. They know exactly where their strengths and weaknesses are. This self-evaluation helps them make better decisions and identifies in what areas they need to grow. It also helps them to maximize their strengths and find potential areas they may need help with. I say learn how to toot your horn! You are special, unique, talented, blessed, and magnificent.

Don't minimize your abilities or dumb yourself down for anyone's benefit. Instead, show others what they can do in their lives because you're doing it in yours. Light the path for others and your true and humble heart will shine through. You were born for greatness. Don't settle for good when you can stretch out for great. The following quote spells it out clearly:

"You are not here merely to make a living. You are here in order to enable the world to live more amply, with greater vision, with a finer spirit of hope and achievement. You are here to enrich the world, and you impoverish yourself if you forget the errand."

—Woodrow Wilson

Inside of you, you know this truth. We all know we are capable of amazing things.

EXERCISE:

Here are some questions to consider:

How have you held yourself back from reaching your full potential?

____

____

____

____

____

What are some things you will say to yourself when you find yourself playing small or dumb so as not to offend others?

____

____

____

____

____

How will manifesting the life of your dreams help others? How will you serve others as a direct result of living your dream?

____

____

____

____

____

Internal negativity can be turned around, and you will need to practice the many tools in this book to make it happen. I'll discuss much more information about specific tools for shifting your thinking later in this book.

TAKING STOCK

> "Without continual growth and progress, such words as improvement, achievement and success have no meaning."
> **—Benjamin Franklin**

Being able to see your strengths and weaknesses is so important, and a great way to do it in a balanced way is to take stock of yourself. Identifying your personal strengths and weaknesses can help you build on your greatest assets and develop and transform your weaknesses into strengths. Constant but steady growth, progress, and improvement create the climate and environment for the achievement and success you desire! You have to become a successful person in order to manifest the successful life you seek.

Nine years ago when my first marriage ended in divorce, I blamed my husband and his choices for the demise of our marriage because I was hurt, angry, and in denial about my own bad behavior. I didn't see at the time that I was at least 50 percent of the problem. When I was finally able to look at my own behavior and take responsibility for my defects in the relationship, it was literally like putting on a new pair of glasses, and believe me, I didn't want to admit what I was seeing. I had been self-centered to the extreme by expecting my ex-husband to fulfill my list of never-ending emotional demands.

Subconsciously, I thought it was his job to make me happy, but unfortunately for us both, that was impossible. Our marriage had been on the rocks for a long time, but neither one of us wanted to admit it. I also found out that one of my biggest strengths in the relationship and relationships in general is that I am fiercely loyal and committed to the people I love. I don't beat myself up for staying in my marriage as long as I did because I stuck it out as long as I felt I could, and for sure, I learned that no one is responsible for my happiness but me. Everyone has his or her own row to hoe. Two unhappy people together don't equal happiness, but when two happy and whole people get together, there is no telling just how fantastic the relationship will be! Don't be afraid to look at your own strengths and weaknesses. While it may be somewhat painful, you will also find out just how great you are!

EXERCISE:

So here is where the gravel meets the road. It's time to take a look at your strengths and the areas that need development.

What are your positive character attributes/your strengths (the good things about you)? Maybe you can start with:

I'm interested in personal development because I'm reading this book.

____

____

____

____

What are some areas you know you still need to develop to help you achieve your amazing life?

____

____

____

____

____

Always keep in mind that we are all works in progress. Life is a journey, not a destination. There really is no "there" to get to. Once we reach our goals, it will be time to create new ones. Isn't this an exciting concept? When we aren't willing to learn new things, we stop growing. Consider yourself a lifelong learner because certainly there is always something new to learn along the way. As you continue on your path, be sure and re-evaluate your strengths and the areas that need development because they will change as you do.

ANXIETY AND FEAR

"Worrying is like a rocking chair; it gives you something to do, but it gets you nowhere."
—Glenn Turner

Did you know that worry and anxiety take a huge toll on your physical health? People who spend a lot of time worrying and experiencing anxiety eventually suffer from heart problems, migraine headaches, and gastrointestinal problems including ulcers, acid reflux, and stomach aches. Worry and anxiety are forms of distress (negative stress) and distress tears down your immune system. Worry and anxiety affect your appetite, sleep, job performance, and relationships, but they can also trigger an increase in unhealthy behaviors like smoking cigarettes, drinking alcohol, or using other drugs.

My close friend Steven had a very stressful and high profile job and was also a single dad of two teenage girls. He often had sleeping problems, suffered from frequent colds and flues, and had frequent stomach aches. Steve shared with me that he often worried about being able to provide adequately for his girls, and that the ongoing quotas he was required to reach at his job caused him moderate to severe (at times) anxiety.

Many nights, he would wake up fearing he would be unable to perform at work and lose his job, and these thoughts and feelings would make him sick to his stomach. He often woke after a night of broken sleep with headaches and emotional hangovers. But when Steve began to practice meditation and relaxation, within just a few weeks, he was sleeping better; he experienced lower stress levels, and as a result, his stomach issues began to improve.

While worry and anxiety are normal reactions to stress, they can become increasingly unmanageable. If you suffer from worry and anxiety, consider practicing these tools to diffuse your stress:

- Identify and acknowledge your worry and anxiety as soon as possible. Don't let them build up to catastrophic levels. Instead, use these new tools to diffuse them before they become unmanageable.
- Practice relaxation techniques. Stop what you are doing and take a time out. Take some deep breaths and remind yourself that you are in charge of your thoughts and feelings. Change the worry channel in your head to something positive, and recognize and affirm that you are only responsible for doing the next indicated thing. Do what you can today, and tomorrow will take care of itself. Remind yourself that a roof is over your head and your feet are on the ground. Take a few more deep breaths and continue with your day.
- Use positive self-talk. Acknowledge that you are feeling worry and anxiety and tell yourself the same things you would tell a close friend. Some examples are:
    - I can do what I can today and let the rest go.
    - Everything will work out because it always does.
    - On a scale of one to ten, how important is it really?
    - I am right here for you and everything will be fine.
    - I am competent and strong and able to handle this effectively.
    - I am surrounded by support.

- Visualization: See yourself moving past the worry and anxiety to peace of mind. How would you look if you were at peace? What would you be doing and saying? Who would be with you? Where would you be? How would peace of mind feel? Spend some time visualizing peacefulness. Take a few deep breaths and move on with your day.

EXERCISE:

What are some tools you already use that are working well for you when you experience worry, anxiety, or fear?

____

____

____

____

____

What are some new tools you can practice when you are experiencing worry, anxiety, or fear?

____

____

____

____

____

What *is* the sense in fearing the future? If you are doing what you can do today to create a better tomorrow, why would you spend what little precious time you have today being fearful about the future? Every action you take today *creates* your tomorrow. Identify and be clear about the goals you've set to create your amazing life and work toward them *today.* Do what you can, when you can, and let the rest go.

Each day is an opportunity for a new beginning to let go of fear and feelings that take away from the creation of your great life. When you find yourself overwhelmed, focusing on your goals and doing what you can do can help you feel accomplished and can shift your focus from worry, fear, and anxiety to hope, achievement, and excitement.

If you go to my website at **OptimistsEdge.com** and click the "Daily Inspiration" link and put in your email address, I will deliver a free daily meditation and quote from my ebook *365 Days to Positive Thinking*. Each day has an important quote, a lesson, an affirmation, and room to share your thoughts about the day. It's a great way to get and stay focused on your goals as you create your amazing life.

MAKING MOUNTAINS OUT OF MOLEHILLS

"Anger is an acid that can do more harm to the vessel in which it is stored than to anything on which it is poured."
—Mark Twain

One day I was driving along a four-lane highway enjoying the sunshine and having a great day. The next thing I knew, a truck pulled up fast and furiously on my right. In it was a red-faced volatile man cursing, yelling, and shaking his fist at me. For the life of me, I could not imagine what I could have done to arouse such anger or to offend him at all. I had now seen anger at its finest, and it really made me reflect on what is and isn't important. I blessed him as he raced off, and I chuckled (just a little) because it seemed so ridiculous to me that he would get SO angry.

Maybe there was more to his story that I don't know, but I have made a commitment to myself first of all to drive friendly. My motto on the road is "merge," which reminds me not to get frustrated and to allow others in whenever possible. Next, I never want to be a red-faced, fist-shaking woman, so I just don't let myself feel too many things are a big deal anymore.

Have you ever seen someone completely blow something out of proportion? One of the best lessons I ever learned was that there aren't really many big deals. A big deal today will most likely not mean a lot tomorrow. Maybe the perceived problem is very important, but usually, it's really not. On a scale of 1-10, 10 being most important, ask yourself, "How important is this problem, situation, or concern?" This question doesn't just apply to your problems but also the problems of others.

Another great question to ask yourself is, "Am I being part of the problem or part of the solution?" If there *is* something you can do to resolve a problem, then take the action and do it. Taking action empowers you to feel accomplished and that you have some control over the negative situation.

If the problem has to do with something outside of your control, maybe practicing some positive activity can take your mind from a negative place back to a positive place so you are no longer focused on the negativity. For example:

- Meditate
- Work out or stretch
- Engage in quiet relaxation while listening to music you love

- Read or go for a walk
- Work in the yard
- Socialize with positive friends
- Journal
- Plan your amazing future—visualize where you would like to be

Practice doing something creative like baking, some kind of art, or something that makes you feel plugged into your spirit like singing, dancing, or meditating. These activities will distract you from the negativity and help you feel positive again. You are much more likely to be able to problem solve effectively when you are in a positive mindset!

Imagine yourself like a lotus flower. Even in a pond, the lotus flower's petals remain dry and untouched because they contain a wax that repels the water. Let the negativity roll off of you. Create a barrier between you and the negativity so you can separate yourself from it. Practice being like the lotus flower.

SUMMARY

Coping with internal and external negativity will take practice, and you will need to be vigilant, but you will also feel so much better as a result! Remember, you are not responsible for the behavior of others, but you are responsible for your own responses so don't get hooked into the negativity of the media and your loved ones, and be ever aware of your own negativity. Take stock of your strengths and weaknesses. You will also need to learn to take constructive criticism and toughen up as you move forward because as you create your amazing life, you will need to gain valuable support from those who are already where you are headed. Sometimes other people can see things about us more clearly than we can see ourselves. Practice your new tools and strategies to reduce anxiety, worry, and fear and press forward. Do your best not to make mountains out of molehills by taking action if you can or by shifting your thinking to something positive if you can't.

Chapter 3

Leaving the Poverty Mindset Behind

"We think sometimes that poverty is only being hungry, naked and homeless. The poverty of being unwanted, unloved and uncared for is the greatest poverty. We must start in our own homes to remedy this kind of poverty."
—Mother Teresa

THE CULTURE OF POVERTY

Thus far, we have discussed internal and external negative thinking (ours and others), tools and strategies to take personal stock and quit limiting our own success, and we have practiced new techniques to cope with limiting thoughts and feelings such as worry, anxiety, and fear, but there are some experiences in life that create negative thoughts and feelings that are harder to shake.

Have you ever experienced poverty that has made you feel unworthy of abundance and success in your life? Have you ever had the persistent fear that you may not have enough money, food, time, or whatever else you think you may need?

When I was in third grade, I remember sitting out on the lunch benches while the kids were eating lunch. I didn't have a lunch. I remember feeling embarrassed and alone. That was a defining moment in my life because I knew in that moment that I was different from the other kids. Although that is the only time I remember not having a lunch to eat at school, there were many times when our utilities were turned off and we didn't have shampoo or much food in the house.

My mother usually worked one or two jobs so she could pay the rent and hopefully have enough money left over to buy food and pay the bills. For the most part, she was a single mom with four kids and had a series of toxic relationships, including men who needed to be taken care of.

From the age of nine until I moved out on my own, I was pretty much the unofficial mediator and physical protector of my mother in her relationship with my second stepdad, who was sometimes violent and a drug abuser. My biggest fear was that if I were unable to intervene because I wasn't home, my mother might be killed. As teenagers, my sister and I, often in the middle of the night, ran to the pay phone up the street to call the police because we feared for my mother's life.

When things were okay, we did all right, but when they were bad, they were awful. The truth is, things were tough, super tough. Altogether, I went to fourteen different schools, and we moved a lot. I can't imagine what that must have been like for my mom, always trying to keep it all together. There wasn't much in the way of help from social services back then, and she was really on her own for the most part.

Despite it all, I feel so fortunate because without doubt, the one thing we all knew was that we were loved. She was always very affectionate and told us frequently that she loved us. Somehow singlehandedly, she always made sure we had a roof over our heads. When I was sick, she would rub my head and bring me milk toast. I remember how proud she was of me when I was little and went through the ceremony to "fly-up" from a bluebird to a campfire girl. She braided my hair extra special that day and stood there smiling right next to me as I lit the candles one by one to celebrate my promotion.

My mother has spent the last thirty years of her life being a cheerleader for all four of us kids; she is an example of what it truly means to "be there" for your family. She has shown up for our weddings, helped us give birth to our babies, and has made it her mission to be the matriarch of our family. She has slept on air mattresses on our living rooms floors when necessary, never complaining, and she has flown from one end of the planet to another so she can be an active part of our lives and the lives of our children. She is the kind of mother I hope to be when my children are grown, and I will always be so grateful for her example of healing, love, and selflessness.

Each of my family members has found his or her own path of healing to some degree, and while we experienced poverty, domestic violence, and addiction, one thing was for sure: We had each other and the love we shared for one another no matter what. We've become exceptional people because of what we experienced. As for myself, I am humbly grateful. I know now that my adversity has given me the ability to love deeply and to have compassion and understanding for others. I chose substance abuse counseling and human services for my professional career, and for the last twenty-plus years, I have been able to share my experience, strength, and hope with others on their paths to healing.

Poverty is generational, and there is much more to poverty than just being broke. Poverty is a culture and mindset. People who live in poverty are conditioned differently than those who have access to enough money and the ability to meet their basic needs. Donna Beegle, an amazing speaker, advocate, and author, is an example of someone who has moved beyond generational poverty to spend her life sharing her story and breaking down poverty stigmas. Her books *See Poverty...Be the Difference* and *Be the Difference: An Action Approach to Educating Students Who Live in the Crisis of Poverty* are giving hope to many and helping people find solutions to complex poverty-related issues.

I related a lot to Beegle's personal story and her ability to connect the dots between poverty and why the people in my life behaved the way they did when I was growing up. Poverty is a learned culture, so it can be unlearned. Along those lines, I have found that prosperity is a learned culture as well. When you know you have the ability to control and create the outcome of your life, you become empowered to recognize what you are capable of and that change is possible.

THE MIRACLE MAN

"Love one another and help others to rise to the higher levels, simply by pouring out love. Love is infectious and the greatest healing energy."

—Sai Baba

Have you ever had an experience where you desperately needed help and someone stepped in and your critical needs were met? Have you ever experienced wellbeing and peace of mind after doing a good deed or practicing an act of kindness?

When we help others, we are helped. When we give to others, we are given everything we need and more. When we can step out of ourselves and really love others, not just through our words but through our actions, we heal and we are healed.

I had an experience two years ago that touched my heart in many ways. I would like to share it with you now. I wrote a short story about it:

Miracle Man

You know there is nothing like a delicious Mexican meal with all the extras like the queso-cheese and refried beans that the waiters bring in the little bowls with the fresh tortilla chips and salsa. In my world, going out to eat on a Friday night with my husband is considered a hot-date night; it is typical once or twice a month, and really, it's all we have time for these days. With teenage boys at home, full-time jobs, finishing up my own college degree and writing a book, we're fortunate to have any downtime at all.

On this typical Friday night, with our bellies full, my husband and I began our short three-mile ride home from the restaurant to begin our weekend. Sometimes the unexpected happens and you encounter situations that hook you, pull you in, and change your life in amazing ways—on this evening, we weren't expecting what would happen next.

Pulling out of the parking lot onto the highway, we saw a man holding a sign. He was older, in his sixties maybe, with a full-beard, kind of frail looking, and his heavy clothes were soiled with what looked like at least a week's worth of dirt. He sat on the ground at the edge of the curb, waving at the cars, but what struck me hardest were the words on his sign: "I NEED A MIRACLE." Could he have said it any clearer? What else could he have said or done to make it more obvious that he was in crisis and that he needed, wanted, and was pleading for help?

I watched people drive by him, staring, reading the sign, and turning away, some appeared disgusted and some were in utter disregard.

Immediately, tears welled up in my eyes. I could feel my husband looking at me—he knows me so well. Neither of us said a word at first, but as we passed the man and turned the corner at the stop sign, I turned and looked at my husband and he said, "Okay, I know, but you can't go back alone." He already knew what I was thinking.

God, I love my husband so much. In that one snapshot of time, I realized once more why I had married him to begin with. You see, he isn't afraid to roll up his sleeves and help, really help. Not help in the way that you cut a check and send it to a company that helps starving children, not that there is anything wrong with that, but help in the way that you aren't afraid to reach out and touch people; really touch them, without fear of getting your hands dirty. I believe that this kind of help was the way of Jesus, Gandhi, Mother Teresa, and many others—the way of love, deep and real love, unconditional love—and I believe it is our responsibility to reach out in this same way to help each other when we can.

I felt a huge rush of gratitude in that moment for all I have: a great job, healthy and smart kids, a home to call my own, a wonderful marriage, and the ability to go out and eat Mexican food on a Friday night. I am warm and safe, and I have a bed to sleep in.

You see, twenty-five years ago, I needed a miracle. There was a time in my life when I wished I were dead, that God would just take me out because I didn't want to wake up for one more day. There were other times when I thought I never should have been born in the first place, that my life was some kind of cruel joke, and that I would never amount to anything. I believed that my lot in life included violence, suffering, and poverty.

We all need miracles at different points in time, such as when we experience the jumping off places—the dark nights of the soul when unanticipated things occur and knock us off our feet into fetal position. Many of us have persevered against incredible odds and our inner light, if not snuffed out altogether, becomes our greatest asset, honing us like gold in a brilliant fire, until we shine and rise from the ashes like a phoenix.

When I needed a miracle most, when I finally held up my sign to speak and ask for help, I was surrounded by family and even some people I didn't know who loved me unconditionally, lifted me up, and made me whole.

So on this Friday night, my husband and I continued driving home, packed up some food and warm clothes and headed back to the man with the sign. I dropped my husband off near the man on the curb, and as I pulled away, I watched my husband sit down on the curb with the man and begin talking. My husband gave the man the food we prepared and some clean, warm clothes (the temperature was in the low forties in Western Washington that evening), and a business card with my name and specific contact information on it. My husband told the man to call me first thing in the morning if he needed help. The man told my husband that he was very apprehensive at first when my husband sat down next to him because he wasn't sure what to make of my husband's attention to him. He said he was just passing through town and was hoping to get back to his family out of state. That was the extent of the conversation, except that the man thanked my husband and expressed gratitude for his help.

The next morning at work, I was standing in the lobby when our receptionist answered the phone. Whoever was on the line asked for me by name; he sounded like an older man, the receptionist said, but she wasn't sure who he was. She put the man on hold until I could pick up the line, which I did within a few seconds, but when I picked up the line, no one was there. I wondered whether it was the Miracle Man. I may never know what happened to him...but I hope for one moment he was able to believe that the world is a good place, a safe place, and that someone, somewhere cared for him. There are Miracle Men, Women, and Children everywhere. Look for them; seek them out and help them in whatever way you can. Regardless of the outcome, we did the right thing, the honorable thing, and the one thing that many of us could do if we chose to. Let's make sure *no one gets left behind.*

In my many years of work in human services, I have been blessed and honored to create and develop three homeless housing programs in my community (Kitsap County, Washington), O'Hana House for homeless women and their children (O'Hana means "family" and that no one gets left behind), The Lighthouse for homeless men, and Forward Bound for high-need homeless families, which in combination, provide more than 25,500 bed nights each year for homeless people with multiple barriers, many of whom are children. I didn't do this alone; I was blessed to have many helping hands and hearts along the way, including a team of unbelievably devoted people who also have histories of adversity and have come out on the other side alive, grateful, and ready and willing to help someone else. I lead an entire team of servant leaders who lift me up, give me strength and hope, and remind me every day of what is most important.

While I have witnessed tragedy in others' lives in the course of my work, I have more importantly learned that, sometimes, all people need is a little hope and a hand up. I have had the joyous privilege of watching people change their lives and overcome severe adversity because someone had faith in them that they could. I have seen them create their own amazing lives and then go out and choose careers where they could help others.

Don't judge someone until you have walked a mile in his or her shoes. Instead, walk alongside others and see how you can help. Shine your light bright for all to see. Don't be afraid to share your strengths with others. You have so much to give, and it is such a simple but profound thing to give your time, love, and attention to those who need it most.

REACHING OUT

"Do what you can, with what you have, where you are."
—Theodore Roosevelt

When I was growing up, I remember it seemed like we always had some stray person or family "temporarily" staying with us. I didn't understand this situation, and as an adult, I judged my mother and considered it bad parenting that she would expose us to potential people who could have been abusive (though I don't recall this ever happening). Besides making our physical space even smaller because there were additional people in it, I also felt that it took away from what minimal things we did have like our food supply, and it probably made it even harder on my mom to provide for us when she had even more mouths to feed.

A couple of years ago, I was sitting at my desk at work thinking about my grandmother. She was a firecracker! She was raised in Unalakleet, Alaska. Let's just say that this is so far north that the Iditarod sled dog race goes straight through the town each year. I have heard stories that my grandmother had to boil ice to get water. Her father was a sled dog mail carrier and reindeer herder, and she was the youngest of five brothers and sisters.

When my grandmother was ten years old, she helped care for her mother until she died of cancer. Instead of being allowed to grieve with her family, for whatever reason, my grandmother and her brothers and sisters were all separated, and my grandmother ended up in an orphanage in Poulsbo, Washington. From the time she was thirteen years old, she cooked on the tugboats. She had a rough life and worked very hard, but she always, always, made room in her home and in her life for others in need, including my mom and we four kids when we had nowhere to go.

Still at my desk, my thoughts traveled to my mother who was always willing to lend a helping hand. When her friends were struggling or when someone needed help, she opened her heart and our home wherever we were, to give of herself and her slender resources.

Still sitting at my desk, it suddenly occurred to me for the first time in my life that I am a third generation helper—first my grandmother, then my mother, and now me. What I considered bad parenting on the part of my mother was actually generosity, hope, and the willingness to go the extra mile to make sure no one gets left behind. Thank you, Mom, for teaching me the value of being there for others when they need you most. You have left me and my sister and brothers an incredible legacy of selflessness and love.

When you give to others, you prosper in more ways than you can imagine at that moment. Whatever your dream is, whatever your amazing life looks like, when you reach that place, give back. Maybe you even have something to contribute now. If so, there is no time like the present to reach out and help someone else.

EXERCISE:

In what ways have you experienced poverty in your life, and how has that affected your ability to prosper in your life today?

____

____

____

____

____

In what ways will you give back when you are able, or now if you can? What are some ideas you have about how you can serve others?

____

____

____

____

____

What legacy have your relatives and caretakers left for you? What can you thank them for modeling and sharing with you in your lifetime?

____

____

____

____

____

What will be the legacy you leave for the people you love in your life? What can you contribute to them as you reach your goals and create your amazing life?

____

____

____

____

____

The best way to banish your poverty mindset permanently is to continue to be aware of everything you have. Notice the language you use about money and abundance. Is there "never enough" or "always more than enough"? If you continue to say there is not enough, then that is what you will experience. If you can see that your basic needs are met and that you have more than enough, if you are willing to reach out to others and share what it is you do have, if you are willing to look on the bright side, you will experience increased abundance in all ways. It is time to let go of your poverty mindset. Remind yourself frequently, "I'm not into poverty anymore!" Remind yourself right now that you have everything you need to succeed inside of you because you do!

ATTITUDE OF GRATITUDE

"Develop an attitude of gratitude, and give thanks for everything that happens to you, knowing that every step forward is a step toward achieving something bigger and better than your current situation."

—Brian Tracy

You can practice gratitude for what you already have and feel blessed and appreciative for it, or you can choose to live in the mindset of scarcity and lack, fearing that you'll never realize your dreams or have what you need and want in your life. Your very future hinges on which you choose and only you can make the choice. Today I am grateful because:

- I have physical, emotional, and spiritual health at this moment
- I am willing to walk through my fears and follow my dreams
- I can hear the birds singing outside
- I can see the faces of my children and the sunset at the end of the day

- I know I will get three healthy meals today and a pillow tonight to lay my head on
- My family is healthy and safe
- I live in the United States where I can be free
- I have people in my life whom I love, and who love me

There is so much to be grateful for—just look around you. As you acknowledge and appreciate all the good in your life, the universe bows to you and makes clear the path that leads you directly to your dreams. Today, I am the richest and happiest person in the world. How about you?

EXERCISE:

What are you grateful for in your life?

___

___

___

___

___

___

___

___

___

___

___

___

___

SUMMARY

As you move forward from here, you will no longer need your old tools. You will find that as you practice using the tools and strategies you have learned so far in this book, you will no longer need to rely on old patterns of thinking, feeling, and behaving. The negativity of your past is done; you have learned how to minimize the internal and external negativity in and around you, and you have learned to leave your old poverty mindset of scarcity and lack behind. You have begun to practice an attitude of gratitude, and you have everything you need and plenty to share with others. With your new perception, keep your new pair of glasses nearby as you continue to move forward and create your amazing life!

Chapter 4
Coping With Change

"Change is the essence of life. Be willing to surrender what you are for whom you could become."
—Anonymous

Do you have difficulty coping with change when it occurs? Do you struggle when things change in midstream? Do you have a hard time being flexible when things don't turn out your way or people don't act how you think they should?

I've had many significant changes in my own life, both exhilarating and crippling, including the loss of my first marriage, death of loved ones, change in careers, graduating from college, and changing my lifestyle choices (the way I eat, recovering from chemical dependency, and quitting smoking), each of which created a wide range of feelings and shifts in my attitudes. The one common theme in all of these changes was *ME*! The more flexible and open-minded I could be, the more I was able to reframe and change my perspective and use each experience as an opportunity for growth.

"Embrace change; it's the one sure thing."
—Robin O'Grady

The loss of my first marriage was the most painful yet cathartic experience ever. It turned my entire life upside down, but in the end, it was the biggest blessing and catalyst for growth and personal development I have ever experienced.

When my first husband and I began having problems thirteen years into our marriage, I was filled with anger and hurt that we could not make it work, and I had never imagined the possibility of divorce until that moment. With two small children we both adored, we separated.

I remember the night he left with his bag packed—I was standing in the living room of the house we had shared, my children asleep, and I felt like my world was over. How would I ever get through this, and what about the kids? This was one curve ball I had just never expected. My entire life had been planned around my children and my marriage. Talk about change! After he was gone that night, my children were tucked in their beds as I slipped to the floor, sobbing in fetal position, and I knew that very night, I was going to go into the abyss. I could not imagine how I would get through it or how my heart would survive. Worse yet, how would I help my kids get through it when I was so hurt myself? For the next two years, I cried a lot. I did my best to continue functioning, and I know that if it had not been for my beautiful children and the necessity to care for them, I might have slipped off the edge into the dark forever.

I had watched people go through divorce over the years, including my own parents, and my perception was that others made it look so easy, at least compared to how I felt on the inside. I felt like I was dying, and in effect, parts of me really were dying. My old inner skin was being sloughed off to make room for the new, though it was difficult to see at the time. I was fortunate to have some close friends who watched over me and who never got tired of me sharing my feelings about my experience and my healing process.

In the beginning, I blamed my husband completely for our relationship's demise. I was very resistant to the change and unwilling to see my part in it, which only fed my self-righteous anger and depression. I had to make some sort of sense of how this situation could have happened. As time went on and I was able to take a real look at the whole picture, I realized clearly that I was 50 percent of the problem. It wasn't about placing blame at all because it didn't matter anyway. Sometimes you just have to accept change. The more I owned my behaviors and rolled with the changes that seemed to be endless at the time, rather than resisting them, the more peace I felt, and the more I was able to let go with love and forgive him.

You see, I was expecting him to make me happy, but the truth was he couldn't win with me no matter what he did. I set our marriage up to fail because I was miserable in my own skin! I had hollow leg syndrome, meaning there was never enough love, attention, sex, recognition, money, or whatever it was that I felt he should have supplied for me. In my mind, he was entirely responsible for my happiness and my emotional wellbeing. I was selfish, self-serving, and unreasonable, and while I loved him with all my heart and gave everything I had inside and out to my marriage and family, there was no way he could meet my incessant demands. My behavior and constant disapproval toward him pushed him toward seeking affirmation outside of our marriage.

Through the use of daily meditation and prayer, including praying specifically for my ex-husband, I was not only able to forgive him for his bad choices, but I was also able to forgive myself for my deficiencies in our marriage. Since then, I have learned valuable lessons about supporting and nurturing a partner and being less sensitive and self-centered in my relationships. I have also learned how to ask for what I need rather than assuming my partner will figure it out and give it to me as though he has a crystal ball.

Recently, my ex-husband married a wonderful woman and they now live close by. Our children know that while Mom and Dad are no longer together and we have moved on in our romantic lives, they are loved and we are all still family. Hindsight is 20/20, isn't it? This is the power of acceptance, and the healing power of love and forgiveness.

Over many years, I have worked diligently on loving and honoring myself, and I am learning how to fill my own needs. I no longer expect anyone else to take responsibility for my joy and happiness. When two whole people come together, they can support and encourage each other and share a great life. When relationships begin on an unequal playing field or when one partner is emotionally unavailable or carrying heavy baggage, disaster ensues.

Learn to fill your own cup and connect with yourself and you will be ready to be an active partner in a healthy relationship. You will have so much more to contribute when you enter a relationship as a whole person rather than counting on someone else to "make you whole."

I was remarried three years ago to a wonderful caring man who has a strong sense of self as I now do. Independently and together, we have great lives, and we thoroughly enjoy our own interests and also our shared interests. Because of the experiences of my first marriage, I have learned so much about myself and being a good partner.

I have also learned the biggest, most helpful lesson of all: *Leave your partner alone!* Something doesn't have to be wrong with the relationship or with him/her all the time. So he's watching "too much" TV; so she's a little messy. Who cares? Go about your business. Quit picking on your partner; let him/her be and do what he/she wants. There doesn't always have to be an issue in the relationship! The more you can allow your partner to be who he is and do his own thing, the more he will feel empowered and valued in the relationship. There is a reason you chose your partner in the first place, and hopefully, it was because you love and admire him and you were attracted to who he was. It's about respect. No one has the right to try and change anyone else, and who is anyone to decide someone else needs to change in the first place? (If the shoe fits, wear it.)

On a different note, change comes more naturally for some people than others. Some people *really* struggle with regaining balance when change occurs. Here are some examples of common changes that create potential unbalance for people. Maybe you can relate to a couple:

- A friend calls and cancels plans to meet you at the last minute
- You go to work with an agenda in mind, but due to unforeseen circumstances, you are unable to do what you planned

- Your car breaks down on the side of the road, and you forgot your cell phone on your dresser at home
- You are about to cook dinner when you realize you have to cook something different than what you planned because you are missing an ingredient
- Your best friends who are married inform you that they are getting a divorce

Human beings are creatures of habit, so is it any wonder we struggle when changes occur? Big or small, for many, the thought of change can illicit feelings of being out of control, especially if you have the illusion that you've been in control in the first place. Change can also create feelings of loss, sadness, and anxiety. It is valuable to learn how to roll with your resistance to change and reframe its meaning to see it in a positive light. Here are some great strategies and a useful exercise to practice that will help you begin rolling with your resistance and reframing change:

- Identify the change. Do some writing about the change to get a new perspective about it.
- Acknowledge your feelings about whatever the change is.
- Identify what fears/concerns come up as a result of the change.
- Identify what effect this change will have in your life.
- Look purposely for the silver lining! When you can attach positive meaning to the change, you can transform your feelings and attitude toward it.

EXERCISE:

Clearly identify what is changing:

Your feelings about this change are:

You are fearful/concerned about this change because:

This change will affect your life in the following ways:

This change may actually be good because:

____

____

____

____

____

____

In what ways will this change provide you with new skill sets? How?

____

____

____

____

____

____

____

To "cope" refers to the thoughts and actions you use to deal with stress. By using the tools mentioned in this book and learning how to manage your stress before it gets out of hand, you will be sufficiently prepared for the changes that will occur as you continue to move forward and create your amazing life.

BE FLEXIBLE

> "Stay committed to your decisions,
> but stay flexible in your approach."
> **—Tony Robbins**

I've been to several seminars and trainings over the years about change that suggested that setting firm boundaries in my life (i.e.

relationships, time management, etc.) would somehow give me the ability to protect myself from the changes occurring in my environment, thereby lessening my stress. For example, I was taught that if you're constantly interrupted at work, let your coworkers know you are only available at a certain time each day, for instance between 8:00 a.m. and 10:00 a.m., and do not deviate from those times. But what I have found is that being flexible is a much better option than setting firm boundaries or becoming rigid about my time because when I am flexible, I am able to move with the change instead of focusing on trying to protect myself from it and being resentful when it doesn't go as I planned.

This flexibility eliminates stress and anxiety. It's true that some boundaries are non-negotiable, but overall, I enjoy change now, and I see it always as an opportunity for personal development. Unless I am working on a project with a non-negotiable timeline, I choose to leave my door open because I am more interested in being available and learning new things than I am about being stressed out because I'm trying to get stuff done and don't want to be interrupted.

CHANGE AND CONTROL

"Letting go doesn't mean that you don't care about someone anymore. It's just realizing that the only person you really have control over is yourself."
—Deborah Reber

Another reason change can be difficult is that some people really struggle with control issues. They believe they have the right or that it is justified to exercise power over the thoughts, feelings, and behaviors of another or over some external circumstance that is actually out of their control. Let's face it: There are some things we can control and some things we can't. Here are some examples:

- **Can Control:** Your own behavior and responses, your thoughts and feelings, your willingness to stay open-minded, your commitment to your own personal growth, your ability to choose positive thinking over negative thinking
- **Can't Control**: The behavior and responses of others, the thoughts and feelings of others, the willingness of others to stay open-minded and committed to their own personal growth, other people's choice to be negative or positive

Do you know that letting go of the illusion of control brings with it great relief? There was a time in my life when I really thought I could control the world from my living room. I knew what *you* needed to do, by gosh, and I was going to tell you just how to do it. This need for control created stress because I felt the weight of the world on my shoulders. What if things didn't go as planned? Not only did I feel responsible for myself, but I felt responsible for everyone else as well. Often, the expectations I had for others were not based on reality and the outcomes I projected did not happen, which set me up for constant disappointment. If only everyone did things my way, the world would be perfect! Wow! Talk about illusions.

Much has been written about Non-interference (Goguen and Meseguer). This concept is also well-known in the self-help community and in the principles of Buddhism. In our short-term gratification society, allowing others just to be who they are, to let them take their time, and to *not* interfere can feel painstaking. It takes practice and patience to let go, to discontinue controlling, and to allow others just to be who they are and to do what they do without us trying to hurry and direct them, but here is the thing: *Control is only an illusion anyway! People do what they want in the end.*

Trying to control, giving unsolicited advice, and manipulating someone to do things your way may initially make it seem like things get done faster, better, and more efficiently because you are in charge, but who likes being told what to do and how to do it? Do you like it when someone tells *you* what you need to do and how you need to do it? Trying to control others causes resentment and repels people from you.

My friends Steph and Robert, who were normally lovely people when they weren't together in the same place at the same time, had some very disastrous dynamics in their relationship. While Robert was somewhat passive, Steph was more of a steamroller, and the combination of the two was painful to watch. Steph constantly picked on and ordered Robert around, and this behavior occurred around other people, friends, and family. To make matters worse, he did whatever she told him with minimal argument, but on the inside, he was like a pressure cooker.

The more she emasculated him and treated him like a child, the further they grew apart, and while he catered to her large menu of demands, he was horribly unhappy. At the same time, Steph was not inclined to treat Robert respectfully because it was not a requirement. Because she felt he did not respect himself, she continued to treat him disrespectfully, and she actually lost respect for him because he tolerated her bad behavior. The harder she pushed, the worse he felt about himself, and the farther apart they grew from one another. She had him convinced he was a horrible handyman, a crappy parent, and an inattentive spouse. How can you expect to be close to someone who treats you that way?

At some point, without serious intervention and action on both parties in a relationship experiencing these dynamics, there becomes just too much water under the bridge and the creation of irreparable damage. Unfortunately, Steph and Robert were not able to work things out, but even worse, unless they are able to heal and change themselves on the inside, it is highly likely they will find themselves in similar relationships.

The practice of not interfering allows others to make their own decisions and mistakes and to experience the consequences of their own behavior, both positive and negative. When we don't interfere, people find out on their own what works best for them and what does not. Non-interference empowers others to recognize that they can successfully make their own choices and that they are capable and competent.

What a relief it is to let people be who they are! You begin to experience peace of mind when you practice allowing and non-interference, and you feel as though you are going *with* the flow of the universe instead of *against* it. Because you are not trying to control another or create a specific outcome, you are free to live in the moment and experience what is happening *right now*. You become a magnet for others because they know you don't have a hidden agenda and they're free to be who they are when they are with you. You'll find you have so much more time and energy to create your amazing life when you are focused on yourself.

Attempting to control is fear-based and self-centered. When you are trying to control people, places, and things, it's because you're fearful that you aren't going to get something you want (your way, your fair share, or some emotional or physical need met), or you're going to lose something you have (a possession, relationship, or some state of being).

CHANGE AND INFLUENCE

"Think twice before you speak, because your words and influence will plant the seed of either success or failure in the mind of another."
—Napoleon Hill

While we may not have direct control over other people, places, and things in general, we are in fact able to influence others. Having influence means the capacity or power to be a compelling force on, or produce effects on, the actions, behaviors, or opinions of others. Therefore, if you have thoughts, feelings, and opinions about something, while it's okay to share them and potentially sway the opinion or feelings in someone else, again the question becomes: Are you trying to manipulate someone or simply trying to get someone to see things your way?

You will need to check out your motives and decide for yourself. If you are someone who struggles with control issues that have hurt you and others, maybe it is better to be happy than right. Let go of the steering wheel if it's not your car! Steer your own car and let others steer theirs.

Change is the natural order of life. A seed lies underneath the dirt, and as it begins to sprout, it eventually pushes through the earth toward the sun. With continued growth, it becomes a bountiful harvest or a mighty oak, and so it is with you. Embrace change because it is the one sure thing! Change is amazing! Change is inspiring! With each small change you make, you widen your perception, you trust your ability to handle life on life's terms, and you grow and learn. You become that bountiful harvest or that mighty oak.

It is also true that as you are creating your amazing life, your dreams, plans, and goals will continue to change. As you live each day creating your life the way you want it, what you want today will probably be very different than what you want two years from now. If you're using the tools and strategies in this book consistently, you'll continue changing and growing from the inside out, and you won't be who you are today two years from now.

SUMMARY

Through the practice of embracing change, remaining flexible, and allowing others to be who they are without your attempts to control them, you will have maximum influence and be in the best possible position to create the changes you want in your own life.

Can't you now see the value in being open to change? Learn to roll with your own resistance to change and you'll experience unshakable strength inside. You'll know that no matter what comes your way, you'll persevere. Now, let the change begin!

Chapter 5
Letting Go of Your Past

"When one door closes, another opens; but we often look so long and so regretfully upon the closed door that we do not see the one which has opened for us."
—Alexander Graham Bell

Have you noticed you spend a lot of time thinking about the past? Does your past haunt you, or keep you distracted from the present or future that you could be creating? Do you have recurring negative thoughts about your past? Do you find yourself rehashing old hurts from your past time and time again?

Leaving the past behind was probably one of the hardest things I ever had to do because it was all I had to hang on to for so long. In the bigger scheme of things, letting go seemed like a monumental task because moving forward meant accepting what had happened to me and forgiving the people who had hurt me so badly. I had no clue where to begin, but I also knew I didn't want to carry the pain and negativity associated with my childhood around anymore because it was affecting my ability to change, heal, and grow as a person.

I had blown my tragedy horn for so long, mostly because I didn't know any other way to function. My history was a crutch and a club. It was a crutch because my past was really all I had to look back on. I didn't have many positive memories so my negative past was the only thing I really had to talk or think about. It was also the club I beat myself up with emotionally, living in the constant downward spiral of "I should have," "I could have," "I would have," and "if only." How could I have lived such a meaningless life all those years, addicted to drugs, treating myself so horribly? How could I have hurt those I loved most so badly and put myself in danger so many times? These were the repetitive questions I flogged myself with day in and day out.

When I chose to live and got sober, I spent all my time with like-minded people with similar backgrounds. At the time, I didn't know the analogy that *water seeks its own level*, meaning that you attract relationships with people who have issues similar to your own. The people I hung out with were sick like me and very new to sobriety themselves.

I had the tendency to focus primarily on the negative in all of my life areas, so I gravitated toward people who also focused on the negative, but as time went on, I started getting healthier and needed to surround myself with people who were healthier. I found myself seeking the companionship of new friends who were growing, changing, and living quality lives. These new relationships were extremely important for me to continue moving forward in my life. If you feel that you're being stifled in your relationships, or if you don't have much in common with the people around you anymore, honor your personal development and begin cultivating new relationships.

I'm not suggesting that you cut people off at the knees or you abandon the people you love. I'm suggesting you seek out people who have the quality of life you want for yourself. These are the people you want to gravitate toward because they'll lift you up and help you reach your goals and find new ways you might not have thought about to create your amazing life.

For myself, I have found many new friends as a result of joining and attending networking groups in my community like Toastmasters International, Soroptimist International, and business networking opportunities such as Rotary Clubs to name a few. Personal development trainings or entrepreneurial groups are also great places to find quality people who are like-minded and want to be their best while making a contribution to the world. I encourage you to seek out these groups in your own community. You will be pleasantly surprised at the people and opportunities you will meet along the way as a result.

EXERCISE:

What are some things about your past that have kept you stuck?

____

____

____

____

____

Have you used your past as a crutch to make excuses for your current life? If so, how?

____

____

____

____

____

Have you used the story of your past to settle for mediocrity out of fear or lack of motivation?

____

____

____

____

____

Which stories from your past do you need to stop telling and let go of so you can move on?

____

____

____

____

____

In what ways have you used your past and past behaviors and choices to beat yourself up?

____

____

____

____

____

Are their certain relationships in your life in which you commiserate and keep your past alive? How can you begin to shift these relationships or let go of them altogether?

____

____

____

____

____

What are some of the characteristics you find attractive in people who are healthy and moving toward their dreams?

____

____

____

____

____

____

Where are some places in your community where you could find quality people, and what are some actions you can take to get to know them better?

____

____

____

____

____

____

GET A COACH OR MENTOR

"Mentoring is a brain to pick, an ear to listen and a push in the right direction."
—John C. Crosby

A mentor is a trusted counselor or guide who has achieved the level of success in his or her life that you want in your own. According to your own definition of success, a mentor might be: someone who has great relationships, a great career, emotional, physical or spiritual wellbeing, a balanced life, financial wealth, or whatever it is you value in the creation of your amazing life.

I have had many incredible mentors over the course of my life whom I hope to continue emulating in all of my life areas, but none stands out more than my current coach and mentor, Patrick Snow. He is an acclaimed international best-selling author, coach, and speaker, and his direction and inspiration continue to propel me forward in reaching my goals and the life I have always dreamed of. Because my path has been similar to his and he has been where I am now and where I plan to go, I have found his feedback, suggestions, experiences, and personal example invaluable, and I am so grateful that I have the opportunity to utilize his expertise.

Finding a coach puts you ahead of the game. There is no need to reinvent the wheel; a coach or mentor can help you shorten your learning curve and get you where you want to be at an accelerated pace. Being a coach and mentor for others has been one of my biggest joys. When you surround yourself with greatness, you are lifted up and inspired to become the very best version of yourself, and you gain the knowledge that other people believe in you and you can do anything you put your mind to.

I am a natural born leader who loves to help others. Part of the creation of my amazing life includes my commitment to share what I have learned with you and personally to help and guide you to accelerate your process in the creation of your amazing life. By joining my Dream Team Coaching Group, you will significantly shorten your learning curve and fill the shoes of greatness in your life.

Let me ask you a few questions to see whether you may be interested. Are you unhappy in your work? Are you tired of financial crises in your life, living paycheck to paycheck? Do you want an accountability partner? Do you want better health, more joy, independence, time, money, and love in your life? Would it benefit you to have someone on your side to guide you, inspire you, and motivate you? Someone who has been where you are and is now where you hope to be one day?

If you answered, "Yes" to any of these questions, I invite you to join my Dream Team Coaching Program. My Dream Team is a community of people who are creating their amazing lives together and reaching the goals and dreams to which they have aspired. They dial into my inspirational call at the beginning of each week to ask important questions and to hear me deliver a live inspirational message directly to club members. The purpose of the call is to help give you that extra dose of inspiration you may need for the week to help you move beyond negativity and reach your goals to create your amazing life.

Each call is one-hour long and includes a forty-five minute presentation and fifteen minutes of question and answer time. You and the other club members can ask anything you want. My goal is to provide you with inspiration, energy, resources, ideas, tools, and strategies to help you identify, create, and take action toward the manifestation of your amazing life.

Each weekly call costs about the same as a cup of coffee and can be accessed 24/7 via my website in case you miss the call. When you join the Dream Team, you will also get some awesome free stuff directly from me.

For more information about my Dream Team Coaching Group, and to join today, visit my website at **OptimistsEdge.com** and click on "Dream Team Community." I look forward to serving you as your personal accountability partner and to helping you create your amazing life.

EXERCISE:

Who have been influential people or unofficial mentors in your life?

____

____

____

____

____

What lessons have you learned from your mentors, and how have you used these lessons in your own life?

____

____

____

____

____

How could a coach help you in the creation of your amazing life now?

SUMMARY

In order to move forward, you will need to let go of your past. Dwelling in the past will keep you stuck in mediocrity, and it is a waste of your valuable time. Instead, look for those who have what you want and seek them out. Find support and new opportunities through local community and networking groups, and for the best possible jumpstart, consider joining my Dream Team Coaching Program. We are ready to help you get where you want to be!

Chapter 6
Learning To Forgive

"To forgive is to set a prisoner free and discover that the prisoner was you."
—Lewis Smedes

The single most powerful tool to positive thinking that I've learned and practiced is the power of forgiveness. When you experience negative situations or you stew on memories of people whom you perceive have done you wrong, hurt you, or created drama in your life in some way, the thought of forgiving them may seem daunting. Forgiveness does not mean that you forget completely about people and situations that have harmed you. Rather, it means that you choose to release the feelings of sadness, fear, hurt, and anger because you don't want to carry around heavy, useless resentments anymore. Forgiveness is about letting go of the toxic re-enactments of your past in your mind and heart.

I will never forget a woman whom I was privileged to hear speak twenty-two years ago. Not only was she brave, courageous, and strong, but she was free from a horrific incident from which most people in her position would possibly never recover. You see, she had been abducted by two men, raped for more than three days, shot in the head, and left in an alley for dead. Yet, she did not die, and she stood before us, talking about the power of forgiveness. When asked how she could possibly forgive her perpetrators, she replied that she was not willing to give them one inch of her attention, time, or energy after what they had taken from her. She said the only choice was to take the high road and forgive them for what they did in order to continue living her life. "No one in his right mind would have made the choices they did," she stated, "so surely they were sick." This woman, for the greater good and for self-preservation, was able to forgive.

When I was younger, I had a lot of resentment about the way I was raised and about things that had happened to me. I didn't really have any tools to release all my anger, so I carried it with me. Because I didn't have any positive outlets to release it, it came out in inappropriate ways and hurt the people I loved.

During a rough time in my healing process, I had a counseling appointment one morning that was really painful. Later that day, I was still reeling from my feelings earlier in the morning as I was driving in the car with my kids. They were in a particularly rambunctious mood that day, and I had asked them a few times to please stop "dinking" around while I was driving because as they escalated their behavior, it was becoming distracting and stressful. Directly after I asked my boys the third time to settle down, my youngest son hurled something toward my older son in the front seat, and it whizzed past my head. Had I been in my right mind, I would've pulled the car over and maturely discussed the potential dangers of what had just happened. Embarrassingly, that was not how I handled the situation.

Instead, I pulled over onto the side of the road and lost my mind. First I yelled in a voice that sounded like a wild banshee, and then for the first time in my children's lives, I broke down and cried. Although I don't normally believe in hiding tears from my children, I was so ashamed of my outburst, so angry that they hadn't listened to me, and so upset about the whole situation, that this time I couldn't hold my feelings back. I was feeling completely powerless, which had been the theme of my counseling session that morning.

My kids were shocked. They had never seen me behave that way (and they haven't since, thank God). I, and they, were quiet the rest of the way home. Later, I was able to apologize and talk to my boys about what had happened. I believe in making amends to those you hurt (and frighten, in my case that day) when you make mistakes, especially to children. They are worthy of respect and deserve love, safety, and consistency.

My sons also apologized for misbehaving in the car. I believe the reason we were all able to take responsibility for our behavior was because I had modeled the importance of accountability from the time they were very small. I forgave them, and they forgave me, but most importantly, I forgave myself. The incident was a huge lesson for me about how not to behave, and for that, I am grateful. I also realized that the real issue for me in this situation was that I had more healing to do. Sometimes our old stuff can get in the way of our new life.

Sometimes forgiveness can take a while. Forgiveness is a process that usually occurs over time, but there are some simple things you can do to make a very good start! Check out the following helpful success strategies to get you started.

HELPFUL SUCCESS STRATEGIES:

If you're able and willing, pray for or meditate on the person you resent every day, and ask that he or she be given all the things you want for yourself. You can do this in your special space that you have designated for the creation of your amazing life (see the section "Starting Your Day on the Right Foot" in Chapter 7) because this process truly is taking charge of your own feelings in an effort to be free from negativity. You don't even have to mean it, but notice what happens after a couple of weeks. You will find you have a completely different perspective on the resentment, and the strong feelings you had will be gone or at least have dissipated.

See and imagine yourself each day as free from the negative emotions around the resentment. What would you be saying or doing as a result of experiencing the freedom of forgiveness? Express gratitude for being free of your resentment. What would that feel like? Act as if forgiveness has already occurred.

Write down your resentment and get rid of it literally. Burn it, send it into space in a balloon, put it in a bottle and send it out to sea, whatever it takes to get it out of you. Rituals such as these can be very symbolic and freeing. For stubborn resentments, you can do a combination of these processes or do them more than once until you find your resentment has much less of a grip on your thoughts and feelings. Being free from your resentments does not mean you forget about them, although this may be the case in many instances, but it does mean that they no longer dictate your thoughts and behavior. You no longer allow them to rent space in your head.

Take the high road. When you feel slighted by others, do your best to let it go. Don't take it personally. Everything isn't about you, and everyone has his or her own perception of what's going on. What would be the loving way to handle the situation? Imagine handling the situation with love, and follow through with positive action if possible. Sometimes handling resentment in a loving way automatically creates feelings of forgiveness because you know you have done your part in taking a proactive and positive approach.

Interestingly, many people have shared with me that they've found that the hardest person to forgive is themselves and they would never tolerate another person treating them as badly as they've treated themselves. If this is the case for you, you owe it to yourself to be kind, compassionate, and forgiving toward you! The same processes above apply to you, and as you practice them each day, notice how much better you begin to feel about yourself, other people and situations, and the whole world. You care enough about yourself to grow past your negativity by reading this book and learning new skills, so what a great start you've made already!

At first, when you practice forgiveness, it may feel insincere, but that's okay. If you continue practicing forgiveness and make it a habit when something or someone causes you upset, you'll be amazed by how light you begin to feel. Little things that you know would have bothered you in the past, maybe even deeply, no longer have the same effect on you. You'll find that you're less connected to the negativity of others and are less likely to get hooked by external negativity when you regularly practice forgiveness.

MAKING AMENDS

"Love in the real world means saying you're
sorry ten times a day."
—Kathie Lee Gifford

Don't be too proud to say you're sorry when you realize you have done something wrong or when someone lets you know you have slighted him in some way. When you make a mistake that affects someone else or you feel you need to make amends for something you have done, make amends immediately. Asking the question, "Do you forgive me?" is powerful and can bring great relief. It's okay to humble yourself to ask someone for his forgiveness when you've done something wrong! It means you are taking personal responsibility for your own behavior. The other person may or may not forgive you, but if you make amends, you have done your part. Then, you can honor that person by giving him the opportunity to forgive you in his way, in his time if he is not willing or able to forgive you right away.

The benefit to you for thinking and acting this way is that you don't have to carry around guilt and resentment anymore. There's no invisible wall creating a barrier between you and someone else. This is freedom and this is forgiveness.

Soon, you'll find yourself becoming less and less concerned with the perceived slights of others and more and more focused on positive things like moving forward to create your amazing life. You'll begin to notice that you forgive others almost automatically and that being able to do so contributes to your serenity, peace of mind, and ability to maintain your positive thinking. You no longer sweat the small stuff, and it feels really good!

EXERCISE:

Do you owe anyone in your life an apology?

____

____

____

____

____

What can you do to make amends? What is your plan?

____

____

____

____

____

A Note of Caution: When you make amends and apologize to someone for something you have done, make sure you are ready to discontinue the behavior. Telling someone you are sorry for something and then continuing the behavior hurts everyone involved. Make sure you are committed to changing your behavior and then do it!

What behaviors are you committed to changing when you make your amends?

____

____

____

____

____

SUMMARY

Forgiveness is about letting go of the energy and power of negative feelings in an effort to move forward. It's about being kind and gentle to *you* by releasing negative feelings and thoughts to make space for positive feelings and thoughts. When you forgive, you no longer carry the ugly seed of resentment. It can no longer harm you and you become free. Be willing to apologize when you're in the wrong. Making amends is another way of releasing negative energy so you don't have to continue to feel guilt for your behavior and you free up your energy for more important and positive things.

Chapter 7
Practicing a Positive Attitude

"If you have a positive attitude and constantly strive to give your best effort, eventually you will overcome your immediate problems and find you are ready for greater challenges."
—Pat Riley

Optimism is a mindset that interprets situations and events as being their best, and in which you ultimately expect the best possible outcome from any given situation. Positive thinkers are action takers. When they have a problem, they take responsibility for finding a solution. They're able to overcome obstacles because they see obstacles as challenges rather than problems. They focus on solutions and consider challenge as an opportunity for personal growth. Optimists exude positivity, and their joy is contagious.

Many times in my work, I have team members ask for my feedback and guidance to help them solve complex challenges. I notice they use crises-oriented language rather than solution-oriented language. They rush into my office exasperated and say things like "We have a huge problem" or "I have a major problem." My response to these announcements has become the same each time. I calmly respond with "Oh, you mean we have a challenge!" I love a good challenge and solving difficult challenges makes me feel accomplished, competent, and proud. My response is an example of how a slight shift in your use of language can minimize the negativity of others and promote solution-oriented positive statements instead.

EXERCISE:

Do you notice yourself using crisis-oriented language? What are some examples?

____

____

____

____

____

How can you shift these examples into solution-oriented positive statements instead?

____

____

____

____

____

When you hear yourself using crisis-oriented language or saying things with negative connotations, stop yourself and reframe what you are trying to say into something positive. The more you practice, the more you'll be aware of it, and the more opportunities you will have to create positive solutions to your challenges.

THE BENEFITS OF POSITIVE THINKING

"Think Positive and Positive Things Will Happen."
—Unknown

Did you know there are endless benefits to positive thinking? With practice, positive thinking will create habitual thinking patterns connected to your core beliefs about yourself, your relationships with others, money, security, and life in general.

A positive attitude can make you feel productive and in charge of your life, and it creates feelings of happiness and peace of mind. It can even lead to the creation of an amazing future—one you may not have been able to visualize or consider when you were focused on your life's negative aspects. Just like negativity breeds negativity, positivity also breeds positivity! Some examples of positive thoughts include:

- I have plenty of (time, money, sex, love, attention, etc.)
- I am enough (I'm strong, abundant, beautiful, smart, etc.)
- I am whole and complete and my challenges have made me even stronger
- I am accountable for my own life, and I set appropriate limits with others
- I am responsible for my own happiness
- I am a good (wife, husband, parent, friend, etc.)
- I am strong and worthy
- People know who I really am and love me
- I express my feelings openly and with care

THE EFFECTS OF YOUR POSITIVE THINKING ON OTHERS

"A positive attitude causes a chain reaction of positive thoughts, events and outcomes. It is a catalyst and it sparks extraordinary results."
—Wade Boggs

I knew a young woman who was so positive! She made me feel so important each time I saw her. I bumped into her maybe three or four times a year, and every time I saw her, she was very excited to see me and would take both of my hands in hers and exclaim, "Oh, Robin! I am so glad to see you. How've you been?" It was not what she said; it was the way she said it—she really meant it! I felt like looking behind me sometimes to make sure she was talking to me!

The last time I saw her she was once again delighted to see me and we chatted briefly for a few minutes and went our separate ways. A few months later, I opened the paper only to see her obituary. She had been thirty-five-years old and had experienced a long battle with cancer. I had no idea! She had never mentioned that she'd been sick, and I felt so sad because I would've loved to tell her how much her positive attitude helped me and how much I appreciated her joyful and contagious spirit.

The lesson for me was to treat everyone like she did—as important and relevant—and I do my best to carry on her legacy by greeting people with joy and really being present. She was a great example of being an optimist. Look for the silver lining. In every situation, there is an opportunity to grow. Look for the positive in every situation no matter how bleak it may appear. Identify it, say it out loud, own it, and spread it around every chance you get.

Some physical advantages linked to positive thinking include lower stress levels in the body, lower depression rates, better physical, emotional, and spiritual health, a longer lifespan, and better coping skills. Scientific evidence points to an increased ability of the immune system to fight off sickness, stress, and disease when people are happy, joyful, and positive overall.

Practicing optimism doesn't mean that you have to act like a Pollyanna every day, and surely you'll find that you still struggle at times with those old negative thinking habits. That is because it takes true cognitive effort and practice to root out negative thinking. Practicing optimism doesn't mean you stick your head in the sand and ignore your responsibilities either, but it does mean that you have an internal sense that all is well despite what is going on around you.

Being a positive thinker takes practice and a commitment to be aware of your own thinking and responses. You will need to look for the positive in each situation and to replace negative responses with positive ones. This process may sound like a tall order, especially if you've spent your lifetime being negative, but as time goes on, it'll become easier and you'll find yourself not only feeling better, but also lifting up those around you with your positivity.

Be willing at first to take two steps forward and one step back because sometimes that is how you'll learn your biggest lessons and how you'll evolve. Getting from point A to point B is rarely a straight line, and there are as many ways to get there as there are people trying. Cut yourself some slack and lighten up. Maybe this will be your first experience in enjoying the ride, or maybe you've spent considerable time being optimistic and enjoying the journey of life. Either way, as you practice more and more letting go of negativity and negative responses, you'll experience an abundance of more joy, more contentment, and more fulfillment than ever before. It'll be as though you've been given a new pair of glasses and a different perspective on how you see the world.

Start this change by becoming aware of your negative thinking and call it what it is. Make the choice to intervene on your own behalf by taking action. Build habits to replace your negative thinking with positive thinking. I refer to this process as the Three A's because it is easy to remember and practice. This process can have an immediate and profound effect on your thinking and behavior:

THE THREE A'S

- **Awareness:** Catch yourself when you find yourself thinking negatively
- **Acknowledge:** Acknowledge that you're being negative and make the choice to do something about it
- **Action:** Take action to interrupt the negativity by doing something positive to counteract it

When you repeatedly practice the Three A's, you'll find yourself automatically shifting your focus when you begin thinking negatively. Here is an example of how the process works:

Suzanne finds herself stuck in traffic once again! "I knew I should have gone the other way! This always happens to me, especially when I'm in a hurry. Dang it!"

Awareness: "Complaining about traffic just makes me more stressed and angry and makes me feel even worse."

Acknowledge: "Being negative about it isn't going to make it any better and there is nothing I can do to change the traffic, so I may as well make the best out of it. What can I do to turn this around?"

Action: (Turns the radio on and finds a good channel.) Oh! I love this song, and I haven't heard it forever! (Turns it up.) I haven't been able to slow down long enough to listen to some good music in a while. What a blessing!

A simple shift in focus can make all the difference in the world.

EXERCISE:

What are some situations that tend to trigger your negative thinking? For example, getting stuck in traffic, long lines at the market, loud people, etc.

____

____

____

____

____

How can you reframe these same situations through the use of the Three A's when your negative thinking is triggered by these events? What are some things you can say to yourself to turn your thinking around to something positive? Give examples:

____

____

____

____

____

Remember practicing optimism is a journey, not a destination. Enjoy the ride and make sure to celebrate your successes along the way!

THREE COMMON STUCK POINTS

"Holding on to anger, resentment and hurt only gives you tense muscles, a headache and a sore jaw from clenching your teeth."
—Joan Lunden

In my work, many people have shared three common negative thinking "stuck points" with me. These stuck points held them hostage and got in the way of their forward growth. Maybe you can relate to these "stuck points" too, which I refer to as the Three R's:

- **Rehashing:** Rehashing is the tendency to think and speak about your past over and over in negative ways. This tendency includes recalling, describing, and stewing time and time again, on negative events that have happened in your life.
- **Resentment:** Holding onto and nurturing grudges and feelings of anger, continuing to blame others over and over for things they have done to you in the past rather than taking personal responsibility for moving on, and being unable/unwilling to let painful issues go.
- **Regret:** Beating yourself up again and again about things you could've, should've, or would've done differently if only _________.
- These stuck points can keep you frozen and stifle your ability to feel optimistic. They zap your emotional and physical energy, and they are the biggest offenders to your joy and emotional freedom.

The Three R's interfere with your ability to recognize and celebrate the good in your life in the present, and any hope you may have for your future. They are toxic to your wellbeing and rob you of valuable energy that you could be using instead to create your amazing life.

EXERCISE:

How have rehashing the past, resentment, and regret affected your life?

____

____

____

____

____

How can the forgiveness tools you learned in this book help you begin moving past these poisonous stuck points?

____

____

____

____

____

How can you change the channel in your head when you find your mind lingering on the Three R's? What thoughts and statements can you use to change the channel in your head to the good news?

____

____

____

____

____

Rehashing the past, resentment, and regret are all toxic. Practice noticing when you are stuck in any one of the Three R's, and over time, you will get more skilled at recognizing and diffusing them right away when they rear their ugly heads.

NEGATIVE PERSONALITY STYLES

"What others think of you is none of your business."
—Unknown

We talked about Schleprock in a prior chapter, but do any of the following negative personality styles feel familiar? Do they remind you of someone you know or can you relate to them personally?

- **The Wet Blanket:** The wet blanket is the person who doesn't know how to play. He's serious to the point of being a kill-joy. He doesn't appreciate having fun, and he finds the fun and playfulness of others annoying. He doesn't laugh at jokes—his own or anyone else's. If you allow him to, the wet blanket will skillfully take the wind out of your sails, and if you have a great idea, he'll be the first to tell you why it won't succeed or work out.
- **The Complainer:** The complainer will find the worst in every situation and be sure to point it out. She loves to talk about her problems and will hold you hostage, giving you every detail of her horrible experiences. She sees the glass half-empty and feels hopeless and victimized. She complains about her health, her family, her job, and anything else she has the opportunity to complain about to anyone and everyone who will listen.

- **The Grump:** The grump gives new meaning to "sweating the small stuff." He's irritated about the long lines, the slow checkout girls, and the crying babies. He's impatient and believes that things should go his way all the time, and when they don't, he thinks he has the right to make everyone else miserable. Grumps are the horn-honkers, the middle finger givers, and those most likely to get into a verbal or physical scuffle over something trivial.

If you identify with any of these personality styles and are ready to move beyond negativity to create your amazing life, understand that the characteristics of these personality styles don't serve you. By consistently practicing the Three A's and letting go of the Three R's, you'll become aware that your behavior and thinking have started to change. You'll also find you're finally in charge of changing the outcomes of your life! What a gift to know now that it is, and always has been, you in charge of your life! So what will you do now?

EXERCISE:

Do you have any of the characteristics of the above personality styles? Which ones do you identify with the most?

____

____

____

____

____

What can you do to begin changing your behavior when you become aware that you're behaving like a wet blanket, a complainer, or a grump?

____

____

____

____

____

Can you see that the above personality styles don't support your positive thinking? They chip away at the foundation you're building to move beyond negativity to create your amazing life. The more you can catch yourself and interrupt your behavior when you find yourself thinking or acting in negative ways, the less you will be inclined to practice them. As motivation speaker Tony Robbins says, "Repetition is the mother of skill," so the more you practice the tools and strategies in this book, the more aware you will become of what you want, who you want to be, and how you will get there.

THE OPTIMIST'S EDGE

"Optimism is the faith that leads to achievement. Nothing can be done without hope and confidence."

—Helen Keller

Optimists have an advantage, an edge, and are found almost everywhere. Optimists are the people smiling in the grocery line while everyone else is complaining. They are the people driving friendly who let you into their lane, the stranger who voluntarily helps you pick up your belongings when you drop them or who holds the door open for you, the customer service person on the phone whose attitude is only improved by crabby, rude people. Optimists are the ones who are looking on the bright side and focusing on what they want—not on what they don't want. They are the people who have that indescribable something in their eyes that emanates outward to everyone they meet. When there is an optimist in the room, everyone knows it.

I will never forget a wonderful woman named Rita, who taught me how to start loving myself and seeing myself with positive eyes and a positive heart. For every negative thing I said to her, she found a way to turn it into something positive. For example, if I said to her "My car broke down and I was stuck on the side of the road for over an hour," she would reply with something like: "Wow, you can be grateful that you own a car to begin with." This kind of response really used to irk me at first because I didn't feel she was listening to me, but in fact, she heard me loud and clear. She was able to turn negative thinking into positive thinking, and eventually over time, I found myself making similar comments to others when I heard them complain.

This last winter, after a severe cold snap, a tree fell down the middle of our house. While this situation was upsetting to say the least, I couldn't help thinking that I'm more fortunate than many in these tough times because I actually have a beautiful home for a tree to fall on.

Rita also had me write a list of the things I liked about myself. This process was very painful for me because I couldn't come up with one thing in the beginning—not one. I remember I sobbed because I realized at that moment just how rotten I felt about myself. Rita then taught me the power of using positive affirmations by suggesting that I write down positive attributes about myself and put them in strategically located places to read aloud when I saw them each day.

One in particular made a huge impact on my self-worth. It simply said, "I love you, Robin" in my very own handwriting and I hung it on my bathroom mirror. At the time, I felt really silly reading it, and honestly, I didn't believe it anyway. At first, I was unable to make eye-contact and look in the mirror at myself while I read it, but eventually, after repeating "I love you, Robin" on several different occasions, I began to look myself in the eyes and even began smiling at myself.

While I used to feel like a liar or conceited about acknowledging and sharing the good things I discovered about myself, I now feel competent, strong, and empowered by my strengths and love to share with others how I was finally able to reconnect with myself.

Using positive affirmations is a great way to begin connecting on an intimate level with yourself. You can turn your negative thoughts into positive ones by owning and accepting the good things about you! As time goes on, you will discover many things to like about yourself. These days, I like to make ridiculous faces at myself in the mirror, and I always chuckle about it because I really do like who I am and it reminds me of just how far I have come and not to take myself so dang seriously.

Be sure to acknowledge the good things about other people too. Isn't that really what everyone wants? Catch someone doing something good and say so! Tell the people around you that you see their positive qualities, and be specific when you mention them. Tell people how much you appreciate and love them. Be positive toward others every chance you get and you'll find that it comes back to you tenfold. Don't miss an opportunity to be helpful or of service to another. Build connections with the people around you, and do your best to acknowledge and accept that everyone is a work in progress and no one is perfect.

When you are optimistic, you become a natural leader. People will gravitate to you because they see in you something that they want for themselves. Being a natural leader means that other people will be watching and emulating you, so behave with integrity. Water the grass where you are standing (more about this later). It isn't always greener on the other side, so do your best in any given situation. By doing so, your positive self-worth blossoms and grows. Remember, you are planting the garden of your future that you'll harvest soon enough. You will be the biggest beneficiary of the results of your own positive thinking.

EXERCISE:

Who are some optimistic people from whom you have learned important lessons?

____

____

____

____

____

What were the lessons you learned and how have they shaped your life?

____

____

____

____

____

How can the use of positive affirmations help you on your path to creating your amazing life?

____

____

____

____

____

Write down ten positive affirmations that you can begin using right away:

1. ____
2. ____
3. ____
4. ____
5. ____
6. ____
7. ____
8. ____
9. ____
10. ____

Carry these affirmations with you and post them where you can see them and read them at least twice a day. I have several on my vision board (I'll explain more about collages and vision boards shortly) where I meditate and pray every morning and one on my bathroom mirror. Begin retraining your mind to identify and acknowledge the great things about you, whether you believe them in the moment or not. Soon, you'll find that you're owning these wonderful affirmations from the inside out, and you'll be able to add many more to your list of the great things about you!

THE POWER OF WORDS

"You can change your world by changing your words.... Remember, death and life are in the power of the tongue."
—Joel Osteen

Did you know that your words have power? Many years ago, I was attending sessions with a wonderful well-meaning therapist. I was in a particularly good mood and feeling strong in one of our sessions, so I remarked enthusiastically that I believed if I wanted to be the President of the United States and began working feverishly to achieve that goal, then I would in fact, achieve it.

The therapist smiled at me and said, "Tsk, tsk, Robin. You really need to accept your limitations." Her words, though not meant to hurt me, completely took the wind out of my sails, and because I wholeheartedly trusted her, I believed what she said and her words stuck with me like a gray cloud over my head. The message I received was: Don't dream too big; don't reach too high because you are limited.

Fast forward to ten years later. I was in session with a client I was counseling when she remarked enthusiastically that she had every intention of getting a great job, regaining custody of not only her son but also her nephew, who was in a bad home environment, and that she was going to purchase a home in a nearby big city. Meaning only the best, I smiled at her and said, "Gosh, I hope you're not biting off more than you can chew, Susan; you really need to accept your limitations." One year later, my client bounced into my office with the good news—with her were her young son, her nephew, and the keys to her new home. She was enrolled in college, had moved to the city, and secured a great job.

Suddenly, while sitting behind my desk, the full realization of what had just occurred hit me like a two by four. How dare I (or my therapist before me) limit the dreams, the success, the motivation, joy, and exuberance of anyone? We do and become what we believe we can do and become. I was so ecstatic for my client and learned such a huge lesson from our experience. Learn to see what *can* be in people and believe them when they tell you what they are capable of doing.

Now, I am here to tell you that there are no limits! You are who and what you say you are—nothing more and nothing less. Walt Disney said, "Dream no small dream!" No one dictates your ability to succeed in your life, only you. You can have, be, or do anything. With each day, with each thought, you determine the outcome of your life. What is considered impossible is only a set of negative limiting beliefs!

Words have the power to hurt, destroy, tear-down, and oppress, and words have the power to heal, create, lift-up, and empower. The words you choose dictate your thinking. How do you speak to yourself? Does your inner voice use kind or destructive words? How do you speak to the people around you? How do you allow other people to speak to you? Begin to listen to those around you. Notice how people in your circle of influence speak—your loved-ones, coworkers, and friends. You can choose to use negative words and perpetuate negativity, or you can choose to use positive words and perpetuate positivity.

GOSSIP IS POISON

"Never make negative comments or spread rumors about anyone. It depreciates their reputation and yours."
—Brian Koslow

Did you know that gossip is the verbal manifestation of negativity in its most insidious form and can cause hurt feelings, broken relationships, and emotional grief to those it affects?

I once worked with a woman who was really brilliant, and I learned so much from her, but toward the end of each conversation, I began to notice she would start gossiping about other people. She'd start the gossiping under the guise that she was really confused or couldn't quite understand why someone would make a particular decision, but then she would really begin to escalate into lambasting the person. I felt very uncomfortable around her, and I started wondering what she was telling other people about me! You can pretty much suspect if someone is gossiping to you about someone else, he or she is also gossiping about you behind your back. Negativity breeds negativity so remove yourself from it and don't participate in it.

Gossip can disguise itself in many ways. It is just like putting lipstick on a pig; despite its outward appearance, it is still a pig nonetheless. Sometimes we can dress gossip up to seem like something else, but it's still gossip. Do any of the following disguises ring true for you?

- Gossip can look like concern when you are using gossip to pretend you know what's best for someone else, including a conversation about someone who isn't present because you're worried about him or you believe you know what is best for him. If you're concerned about someone, why not talk to him directly? Wouldn't you want the same courtesy?
- Gossip can also be the conversation you're having about someone not present "just to vent your feelings." Open communication involves being accountable for your own feelings and expressing them in a mature and direct way. What if you went directly to the person and told him how you felt instead? This conversation gives him the opportunity to own his part in the situation (or not); either way, at least you're treating him with respect and giving him the benefit of the doubt rather than assuming the worst.
- Gossip can be mean-spirited. Some people gossip because they don't feel good about themselves and by gossiping about someone else, they temporarily get the satisfaction of feeling superior, but the truth is they don't feel superior on the inside. People who gossip about others have low self-worth and use gossip as a tool to build themselves up to feel better at others' expense.

- Gossiping can make you feel temporarily closer to or bonded with others who gossip, or it can make you feel like you fit in, but in the long run, it's hurtful, unbecoming, and self-deprecating. The question to ask yourself is, "Who do you want to fit in *with*?"

EXERCISE:

Do you find yourself participating in conversations that include gossip or having conversations with other people who are gossiping?

____

____

____

____

____

Have you ever been the recipient of someone else's gossip? How did that make you feel?

____

____

____

____

____

When you become aware that you're in a conversation that includes gossip, what are some ideas about how you can discontinue the conversation?

____

____

____

____

____

Gossip includes any conversation in which you're discussing someone who isn't present. Do your best not to get involved with the negativity of gossip, and don't gossip yourself because it'll only come back to harm you by making you feel bad about yourself. End conversations or change the subject when you find they are moving in that direction. The end result will be that you get to feel good about yourself, inside and out.

When people know that you don't speak unkindly of others, you become trustworthy because you are modeling trustworthiness and personal integrity. Making a commitment to *yourself* not to participate in gossiping behavior can really give you a self-esteem boost. Learn to change the subject or end the conversation and you will feel better about you.

One effective way I found to discontinue gossiping or listening to gossip when I find myself in situations where gossip is present is simply to say, "I feel like I'm gossiping and I don't like it. Let's move on." This response has never failed me, and no one to my knowledge has ever been offended by it when I said it. It is hard to argue with the truth, and one fundamental truth that is obvious to most is that gossip is hurtful. Do your best not to be a part of it.

HANDS-ON TOOLS FOR CHANGE

"To exist is to change, to change is to mature, to mature is to go on creating oneself endlessly."

—Henri Bergson

CHANGING THE CHANNEL

When you find yourself thinking negatively, make a conscious decision to change the channel. You can even make a comment to yourself like "Thank you for sharing; now be quiet." Envision yourself changing the television channel in your head to the good news. Immediately divert your negative attention to something positive.

For example, you can immediately shift your focus to something you enjoy or love such as a song, a poem, a happy memory, or people you love, your children, your spouse, your mother, or your best friend. Think of something funny, anything to change the negative thought to a positive one. You may find yourself chuckling at the thought of changing the channel in your head, which could be enough in itself to shift your focus.

Changing the channel can also be really helpful if you have difficulty falling asleep because of worry, anxiety, or fear. The more attention you give to positive thoughts, the better you will begin to feel.

GOING WITH THE FLOW

"Flow with whatever may happen and let your mind be free.
Stay centered by accepting whatever you are doing.
This is the ultimate."
—Chuang-Tzu

There really is validity in letting go of struggle and accepting things as they are. Going with the flow means that you do what you can to handle the day-to-day details of your life and then let go. Make your plans, do your footwork, and then leave the outcome to the universe. Going with the flow can be a huge relief for those who are in the habit of controlling everything.

It takes a lot of energy to maintain the illusion that you run the planet, so when you do what you can do and finally let go of the results and everything still turns out okay, it can be a very liberating experience. When you go with the flow, you also give other people the opportunity to grow because you are no longer trying to manage their lives, and they begin to find they are absolutely capable of managing their lives on their own. (Maybe they already knew this anyway.) Imagine that! Going with the flow doesn't mean you can't be helpful; in fact, we all need love and support from those we care about. It means simply that we let go of the reins of the world and narrow our focus down to what is right in front of us.

When we go with the flow, we begin to develop a sense that all is well. That is faith! Faith is the trust in or sincerity of your intentions. If your intentions are to move beyond your negative thinking and live for greatness, then going with the flow can help you move and grow with change rather than buck it and move against it.

HELPFUL SUCCESS STRATEGIES:

- **Realize there is no way humanly possible to control everything:** For instance, you may be able to control what you cook for dinner or what time you plan on showing up to meet a friend, but you can't control your stove if it breaks down while you're cooking, or if you get stood up because your friend has an emergency and can't show up when agreed.
- **Put on your new pair of glasses:** Get a new perspective on the situation. Use the other tools you have learned in this

book to cope with the feeling of being out of control. For instance, when getting stuck in a horrible traffic jam, use that time to listen to some beautiful music or a great audio CD, or recognize that maybe you are getting an important message to slow down in your life. Change your perspective and you'll notice your attitude and feelings about the situation changing too.

- **Be gentle with yourself**: If you are in the habit of thinking you're in control of everything, don't be surprised if letting go is difficult for you. Breathe, have a good laugh, and cut yourself some slack. Positive change takes time and practice, and becoming aware of your need to control is the first step in going with the flow! Use the Three A's that you learned about earlier in this chapter to turn it around! It makes perfect sense that once you are aware of something, you can then begin changing it!
- **Keep a journal:** Something magical happens between the heart and the pen that does not happen between the mind and the mouth. Writing out your thoughts and feelings can help you diffuse negative feelings and shed light on the real issue at hand. Many people have told me that journaling is a very effective tool for finding out what is standing in the way between them and their ability to move forward in their lives. Write out the details of what you're thinking and feeling and maybe even share it with a friend or loved one to get feedback if you're open-minded and would find it useful.

The more you can roll with whatever comes your way, the better and more peaceful you will feel. It is good to dream, set goals, and take action, but don't forget to enjoy what is right in front of you. You don't want to miss out on something important because you're too busy trying to control the outcomes of your plans. Go with the flow and use the other tools and strategies in this book and they will contribute to your wellbeing.

STARTING YOUR DAY ON THE RIGHT FOOT

"If you don't think every day is a good day, just try missing one."
—Cavett Robert

Starting your day on the right foot is a choice. You can choose to hit the ground running by hitting the snooze button on your clock twice without any thought of how you'll create your day, or you can choose to take a few moments to think your day through and make sure you have the time you need to be prepared. As simple as it may sound, being prepared can make the difference between waking up on the wrong side of the bed and having a bad day, or feeling centered and ready to face what comes your way. Being prepared may mean planning ahead by packing your lunch or showering the night before, but it is well-worth your peace of mind. In the morning, while you are still lying in bed, ask yourself these four simple questions:

- What are my plans today?
- How do I want this day to go?
- What are some things I am grateful for today?
- What can I do for someone else today?

Imagine yourself moving through your day cheerfully from room to room, person to person. See yourself enjoying your day and imagine the peace of mind you're feeling as you go about your tasks. Notice how good these thoughts make you feel and then begin your day.

If you find yourself experiencing stress or anxiety over the course of the day or losing your connection with your own peace of mind, find a quiet place to regroup and consider this:

- **You can start your day over right this minute:** Did you know that you can begin your day over any time? If you woke up on the wrong side of the bed or are just having a bad day, you can stop, take a breath, and make the declaration to yourself that you're beginning your day again. You can do this anytime, anywhere, and you can do this several times a day if needed.
- **All you need to do is the next indicated thing, the best way you can:** What a relief to know that you only have to do what is right in front of you right now. Do the best you can at performing the task at hand and you'll notice that you begin to feel better. No need to worry about the tasks of later today or tomorrow because they will take care of themselves later today or tomorrow! For now, do the next indicated thing, the best way you can.
- **Nothing can happen that you won't be able to handle:** You have the ability, the strength, and the support to handle anything that comes your way. You've been handling it this long, and surely you will continue to handle it. If something overwhelming comes your way, you'll have all you need at that time to do whatever it is you need to do.

- **All is well:** Right now, your feet are on the ground, there is a roof over your head, your heart is beating, and you are okay.
- **Go with the flow:** You do not need to struggle if things are not going your way. Relax, take a deep breath, and stay in the moment. Roll with your own resistance and just let it go.

HELPFUL SUCCESS STRATEGIES:

- **Enjoy the ride:** When was the last time you had a good laugh? Do you spend the majority of your time being serious to the point of causing stress? Lighten up! Look for the humor in situations.
- **Find your spirit:** What makes you feel whole and amazing? Is it spending time in nature that makes you feel connected? Listening to beautiful or energizing music? Praying and/or meditating? Find your sun-spot and nurture it every day. Make a commitment to spend twenty minutes a day doing one thing that contributes to the wellbeing of your spirit.
- **Designate a space in your house for meditation and/or prayer**: Find a corner, spot, or area in your home where you can begin developing your amazing life. Commit to spending twenty minutes a day in this space, connecting to your spirit and thinking about what you most desire until it becomes crystal clear.
- **Make a vision board:** If you are a visual person, make a collage or vision board. Clip pictures from books or magazines that represent the direction you are going in your life, your hopes, dreams, and aspirations, and place them on a cork board or a large poster board in an area where you spend a lot

of time. Affirm your intentions by hand-writing notes of affirmation to yourself and placing them on your board. Look at your vision board often to remind yourself of where you are, and where you are going as you create your amazing life.

- **Eat healthy:** Crappy food makes your body feel crappy. Consider making one small change in your diet to help you become healthier. Does sugar make you feel lethargic? Are you eating enough fresh fruits and vegetables? Consider how your current diet affects your overall health and your energy level.
- **Take time to dress your best:** When you dress well, you automatically feel better, you look more professional, and you experience an increased self-worth. You're worth it, so treat yourself accordingly by dressing well.
- **Clean your space:** Your outside space may very well be a metaphor and reflection of where you are on the inside. Cleaning your space provides you with a sense of wellbeing and control over your environment, and it may give you the extra motivation you need to forge ahead.
- **Use positive words:** Practice positive self-talk. If you find yourself thinking negative thoughts or using negative self-talk, change the channel to the good news and turn it around.
- **Write love notes to yourself and/or leave yourself positive and affirming phone messages:** Make 3 x 5 cards with important affirmations that you can repeat and practice. Post them in plain view in places you frequently spend time and know you will see them.

- **Keep good company:** Make the effort to gravitate toward those people in your life who are positive and supportive of your goals. Minimize or discontinue the time you spend with those who zap your energy with negativity whenever possible. When people begin catastrophizing, dramatizing, or speaking negatively, politely change the subject to something positive.
- **Release negative people with love:** If you have friends you avoid or are repelled by because they are negative and are constantly discussing their horrible perception of the world, their bad health, bad relationships, etc., let them go with love. Believe me; it won't be long before they find someone else to dump their garbage on. I know letting people go may sound really mean, especially because I've met some really good-hearted people who were very negative, but truth be told, we attract what we are, and if your plan is to move beyond your negative thinking, you'll at least need to minimize your exposure to negative people.

MEDITATION AND PRAYER

"When you meditate or pray...both are forms of meditation... you give up control and find the answer and you open yourself to receive God's gift, the universal force, or whatever that is."
—Erin Gray

It is noteworthy to mention meditation and prayer again. Meditation and prayer can be a huge catalyst to relieving stress and providing mental clarity of thought. A wonderful woman named

Nancy told me once that there are three rules to meditation and prayer:

1. Perseverance
2. Perseverance
3. Perseverance

You just do it no matter what, whether you feel like it or believe in it, and there is no wrong way to do it. If you've never spent time in meditation or prayer, don't let any prior biases keep you from trying something new. If you have tried one of them before but didn't feel you benefitted from it, stay open-minded. You are making important changes in your life, and while it may take some practice, it may also very well be the best tool you ever give yourself. Try it again and give it ninety days to see what happens. Just 15-20 minutes each morning when you start your day could make a huge difference.

You can meditate and pray in a space you designate to start your day on the right foot, or maybe you would be more comfortable outside or on your bed. There is no wrong way to meditate or pray; many people have reported to me that they meditate and pray in the shower, in their vehicles on the way to work, in their backyards, or in some other place where they felt inclined to do so. It isn't the act as much as it is the intention. You can get quiet for a few moments, read some inspirational material if you choose, close your eyes, and think through your day. If recurring intrusive or random thoughts come to you, notice them, let them go, and get quiet again.

You'll find as time goes on, you may need twenty or even thirty minutes or more in the morning as you continue growing. New ideas and inspiration will come to you often unexpectedly and you will feel energized and inspired. You will begin to look forward to this time each day, knowing that it will help you feel good, stay centered, and keep you focused on the tasks at hand.

After seven years of meditating and praying in the morning prior to starting my day, I really look forward to going to my special place each morning, and I count on this time to help get centered and focused and to put me in a loving and productive frame of mind. I crave this time and feel out of balance if I have to miss out on it. The majority of my epiphanies, spiritual experiences, ideas, and moments of extreme gratitude have come to me during this quiet time, and I believe it has had much to do with inspiring me to press forward with this book's completion and my unceasing commitment to create my amazing life.

By this point in this book, you have hopefully begun to:

- Understand and overcome your negative thinking
- Leave your thoughts of scarcity, lack, and poverty behind you
- Practice new skills and strategies for coping with change
- Learn and practice new skills to forgive others and yourself and grow past resentment and regret
- Learn and practice new skills and strategies for positive thinking

One of the biggest barriers between you and what you want to create in your life is your perception. In the next chapter, we will talk about how to turn your liabilities into assets by identifying your challenges and seeing how they have been your most profound opportunities for growth.

EXERCISE:

How can starting your day on the right foot help you? What will you gain as a result?

____

____

____

____

____

What will you do to ensure you have enough time each day to start your day on the right foot?

____

____

____

____

____

What specific actions will you take in the process of starting your day on the right foot?

____

____

____

____

____

There is no better or faster way to create change in your life than practicing new tools and strategies, and adopting a new routine that supports your dreams and helps you clarify your goals. You deserve to have time for yourself each day to reflect, dream, and set goals, and when you make this commitment to yourself, you'll no longer be living by default. Instead, you will be an active creator and participant in your new amazing life. The results I have had as a result of practicing the tools and strategies in this chapter are ineffable. I encourage you to try them all, mix and match them, and consistently practice the ones that feel right for you. I would love to hear you share about your journey along the way, and I am open to comments from you about how these many tools have helped you. Feel free to email me at **robinogrady@wavecable.com** or visit my website at **OptimistsEdge.com** and click on the "Comment" button. In the next chapter, you will find out how the hardest times in your life are in fact your greatest assets in the creation of your new amazing life.

Chapter 8
Turning Your Coal Into Diamonds

"All misfortune is but a stepping stone to fortune."
—Henry David Thoreau

In this chapter, you will learn strategies for turning your coal into diamonds, i.e. turning the tough times in your life into your biggest strengths. I will give you real life examples of how to change your perception and attach positive meaning to adversity.

You have a life story—we all do—and what you've experienced in your history has helped you write the story of your life up until now. Did you know that your experiences with adversity—the worst and toughest times in your life—are indeed your biggest assets? The definition of adversity is: a state of hardship or affliction; misfortune or a calamitous event. I'll never forget the day I was driving in my car when I realized that all of the things I had been through in the past (the good, the bad, and the ugly) gave me incredible character and made me the amazing person I am today! The adversity I experienced in my past has made me passionate, empathetic, and strong! Here are some examples of how I have turned *my* coal into diamonds:

A) Coal: Because we moved so often while I was growing up, I went to fourteen different schools. It was difficult; I spent a lot of time sad and lonely because I was always the new kid. I didn't want to make friends because I knew we probably wouldn't be staying long anyway.

For a moment, let's take a look at what I learned from those experiences and how those experiences have shaped my new amazing life. Pay special attention to how I have reframed the negative events into positive learning experiences that benefit me now in my life.

Diamond: Because we were constantly moving, I experienced many different cultures and places. I learned to fit in just about anywhere, and I get along with many types of people. Now in my life, roots are very important, and I love being a part of my community. My beautiful children have had a stable childhood and lifelong friends because I didn't want them to experience what I did. It brings me great joy to see people I know in the market, at the bank, and around town in our small town. Each year, I have rituals in my home that I never got to experience growing up. For instance, in the fall, I bring in the hummingbird feeders and my front lawn disappears under a pile of leaves that will need to be raked. I bring into my shop all my potted plants that won't survive the winter. In the spring, the bulbs that I've planted will surface once again, stretching their way toward the sun. These are the diamonds I get to experience now as a result of my need to create stability. Because of the instability of my environment growing up, it has been important for me to create stability. I have learned the valuable lesson of how it feels to "come home."

B) Coal: I experienced domestic violence, trauma, and uncertainty growing up. I was often fearful, and I felt powerless; I had no control over my own safety or the safety of the family members I loved most. This lack of power was frightening and I was never sure what was going to happen next.

Diamond: I'm resilient and strong, and I'm fiercely loyal, protective, and nurturing to my children and those I love. Their safety and security is a priority, and I pay attention to their needs based on my parental responsibilities and good judgment. I treat all people with dignity and respect, and I support and set healthy boundaries around my own safety. It's important for me to have a loving, safe, and reciprocal relationship with my husband based on respect, common values, and our personal beliefs and boundaries about gender roles and the meaning of having a healthy relationship. These diamonds have helped me become a great mom, partner, and friend.

C) Coal: I became addicted to drugs, had no regard for myself or those around me, and participated in self-centered, self-defeating, and self-deprecating thinking and behavior.

Diamond: Now that I have recovered, my own self-care is a priority. I respect myself, love myself, and treat myself as I would a good friend. I don't participate in behaviors or relationships that are hurtful. I focus on how far I've come, and what my wonderful future holds in store for me as I create my amazing life. These are the diamonds that have helped me identify that I am strong and worthy, and that I am a miracle and in charge of my own destiny.

The following "My Old Story" exercise will help you turn your own coal into diamonds by identifying experiences that have kept you stuck, and reframing them in a way that reflects their value to your personal development. By identifying these experiences, you'll be able to see how each experience, no matter how negative, has helped you to be the amazing person you are today. Feel free to use my previous examples as a guide to your own, and remember, this exercise has no right or wrong answers.

YOUR OLD STORY

"Study the past if you would define the future."
—Confucius

This exercise's purpose is to identify significant events, positive and negative, that have shaped your thinking and behaviors to function in the way you presently do. When writing out your significant events, don't censor yourself or be concerned about penmanship; just let your pen do the talking. After completing each section, reflect on your significant events, identifying both the coal and the diamond of the event.

A.) To the best of your recollection, what were the significant events (both negative and positive) that occurred in your life between the ages of 0-10?

Events: ____

____

Coal: ____

Diamond: ____

B.) To the best of your recollection, what were the significant events (both negative and positive) that occurred in your life between the ages of 11-20?

Events: ____

____

Coal: ____

Diamond: ____

C.) To the best of your recollection, what were the significant events (both negative and positive) that occurred in your life between the ages of 21-30?

Events: ____

____

Coal: ____

Diamond: ____

D.) To the best of your recollection, what were the significant events (both negative and positive) that occurred in your life between the ages of 31-40?

Events: ____

____

Coal: ____

Diamond: ____

E.) To the best of your recollection, what were the significant events (both negative and positive) that occurred in your life between the ages of 41-50?

Events: ______________________________

____

Coal: ______________________________

Diamond: ______________________________

F.) To the best of your recollection, what were the significant events (both negative and positive) that occurred in your life between the ages of 51-60+?

Events: ______________________________

____

Coal: ______________________________

Diamond: ______________________________

SUMMARY

Now, can you effectively see your past for what it was and take full responsibility for your present and future? Doing so is the springboard of real change! When you can identify the silver lining in all situations, there is no room left inside you for dwelling on the past, harboring resentment, or blaming others for your circumstances. Then, you can practice forgiveness fully, joyfully, and with complete abandon. Grab your new life with both hands and be free of your own negative limitations, beliefs, and behaviors! Put on your new pair of glasses now and see your life, the world, and everything in it in a different light.

Make room for positivity in your life by opening your heart to the positive. Focus on the positive, be grateful for the positive, and don't forget to count your blessings, however simple they may be. You are amazing and are taking charge of creating the life you've been dreaming of, your new amazing life. Now that you're aware of how your adversity laid the groundwork that brought out the best in you, it is time to identify what you truly want for your future!

Chapter 9
Telling Your New Story

"The best years of your life are the ones in which you decide your problems are your own. You do not blame them on your mother, the ecology, or the president. You realize that you control your own destiny."
—Albert Ellis

It's time to tell your new story and to let your old story go. Let's start by identifying what you really want because as you create your new life by setting goals and taking action, you'll no longer be focusing on what you don't want or on your past; instead, you will be focusing on what you do want, where you are now, and your hopes and dreams for the future.

Who are you? What do you love? What makes you feel alive? These are all questions to ask yourself. You, and only you, are the creator of your future. Your whole life it has been you creating your reality all along. Your beliefs, your thinking, and the actions you've taken have brought you to the place where you are now.

When you think of yourself as happy, joyous, and fulfilled, what does that picture look like? What does that picture feel like? Think about your life areas: love, work, relationships, parenting, recreation, and your social and spiritual lives. What would a successful, balanced life look like to you? How would you spend your time? What would you be doing? Take some time now to answer the following questions that will help you begin to assess and define what you really want.

EXERCISE:

Work

What is your heart's desire in terms of work?

____

____

____

____

____

What kind of work feeds your spirit? Are you a people person, an animal person, a computer whiz?

____

____

____

____

____

What are your career strengths? Weaknesses?

____

____

____

____

____

When you think about a dream job, what does it look like? What would you be doing?

____

____

____

____

____

Relationships

Are you in a meaningful relationship now? What is good or not so good about it?

____

____

____

____

____

What do you have to offer a relationship? What can you bring to the table?

____

____

____

____

____

What are your relationship strengths? Weaknesses?

____

____

____

____

____

What are you hoping to find in a partner and relationship?

If you had your dream relationship, what would it look like?

Social Life

Do you have a small or large social circle? Are you satisfied and content with your social life?

Do you tend to be very social and outgoing or do you prefer a smaller intimate group of friends to share your time with?

Do you have difficulty making friends or nurturing your relationships with friends?

What are your social interests? What types of social activities do you enjoy?

What would your ideal social life look like?

Parenting

Are you happy with the parenting you provide to your children?

What are your parenting strengths and weaknesses?

____

____

____

____

____

____

Do you practice self-care, or are you frequently overwhelmed or do you feel burnt-out? What are some ways you can take care of yourself when you begin to feel this way? What are some things you can do to take care of yourself?

____

____

____

____

____

____

Were your basic needs met by your parents while you were growing up? If not, how has this changed your perception as a parent with your children?

____

____

____

____

____

____

If you were parenting at your optimum level more often, what would that look like?

Recreation

What are you favorite recreational activities, exercises, and sports? Do you make time for recreational activities, exercise, or sports?

What are some recreational activities that you currently enjoy or have enjoyed in the past?

Are there recreational activities that you are interested in and would like to try?

How would exercise benefit you physically and emotionally, and how would it contribute to the creation of your amazing life?

What would a satisfying recreational life look like?

Spiritual

Do you have the desire to or do you already participate in spiritual practices?

Is church, meditation, yoga, prayer, or any other practice important to you?

Do you think that participating in some sort of spiritual practice may benefit you? Why or why not?

____

____

____

____

____

What types of spiritual practices do you find interesting and would you potentially like to learn more about?

____

____

____

____

____

What would be your idea of your best spiritual self? What would that look like?

____

____

____

____

____

The purpose of the previous exercise was to begin identifying and clarifying what is most important to you and what you truly desire. Using the above information as a starting point, you will now develop a specific plan of action and begin making permanent and supportive changes to create the life you have always wanted. By combining the new positive tools and strategies you learned in this book's prior chapters with the daily action you will develop in this chapter, you'll create powerful results that will affirm and empower you to continue moving forward. Identify and describe what daily actions you'll take each day to create your amazing life in the following areas:

My ideal work life would look like:

Examples: I will check the employment section of the paper on Sundays to begin researching other jobs. I will meditate in the morning and imagine myself showing up for work at my current job with a positive attitude.

Three short-term things I can do in the next week to create my ideal work life are:

1. ______________________________
2. ______________________________
3. ______________________________

Three things I will do in the next month to create my ideal work life are:

1. ______________________________
2. ______________________________
3. ______________________________

Three long-term things I will do in the next year to create my ideal work life are:

1. ______________________________
2. ______________________________
3. ______________________________

My ideal relationship would look like:

Examples: I will find a good book on relationships and read it for fifteen minutes each night, and I will take an online communication class.

Three short-term things I can do in the next week to create my ideal relationships are:

1. ______________________________
2. ______________________________
3. ______________________________

Three things I will do in the next month to create my ideal relationships are:

1. ______________________________
2. ______________________________
3. ______________________________

Three long-term things I will do in the next year to create my ideal relationships are:

1. ______________________________
2. ______________________________
3. ______________________________

My ideal social life would look like:

Examples: Make one phone call a day/week to a friend. Choose one day a week to go to lunch or a movie with a friend.

Three short-term things I can do in the next week to create my ideal social life are:

1. ______________________________
2. ______________________________
3. ______________________________

Three things I will do in the next month to create my ideal social life are:

1. ______________________________
2. ______________________________
3. ______________________________

Three long-term things I will do in the next year to create my ideal social life are:

1. ______________________________
2. ______________________________
3. ______________________________

My ideal recreational life would look like:

Examples: I will walk around the block three times a week. I will plan a camping trip.

Three short-term things I can do in the next week to create my ideal recreational life are:

1. ______________________________
2. ______________________________
3. ______________________________

Three things I will do in the next month to create my ideal recreational life are:

1. ______________________________
2. ______________________________
3. ______________________________

Three long-term things I will do in the next year to create my ideal recreational life are:

1. ______________________________
2. ______________________________
3. ______________________________

My ideal parenting life would look like:

Examples: I will spend twenty minutes alone with each of my children at night to tuck them in. I will read a book about effective parenting. I will plan a once a week activity that I know the kids will enjoy.

Three short-term things I can do in the next week to create my ideal parenting life are:

1. ______________________________

2. ______________________________

3. ______________________________

Three things I will do in the next month to create my ideal parenting life are:

1. ______________________________

2. ______________________________

3. ______________________________

Three long-term things I will do in the next year to create my ideal parenting life are:

1. ______________________________

2. ______________________________

3. ______________________________

My ideal family life would look like:

Examples: We will eat dinner together as a family, play a game as a family once a week, or participate in some other activity together.

Three short-term things I can do in the next week to create my ideal family life are:

1. ______________________________

2. ______________________________

3. ______________________________

Three things I will do in the next month to create my ideal family life are:

1. ______________________________
2. ______________________________
3. ______________________________

Three long-term things I will do in the next year to create my ideal family life are:

1. ______________________________
2. ______________________________
3. ______________________________

YOUR PERSONAL MISSION STATEMENT

Identifying what you really want and setting out on a specific course of action to get it gives you purpose and direction and is a huge motivator, but even more importantly, it's a call to action. It's your personal benchmark or measurement tool to determine whether you're on the right track in the creation of your amazing life. Here's an example of a personal mission statement:

> My personal mission is to educate, inspire and motivate as many people as I can through the use of my personal experiences and talents, and to fully participate in my health, my spiritual progress, and my relationships with my family and friends while becoming the very best that I can be.

Reviewing the information that you have identified in your ideal life areas, what is your personal mission statement? Your personal mission statement should be clear and concise and should encapsulate in a nutshell what you identified that you'll create in your life.

My personal mission is to:

____

____

____

____

____

____

____

Review your personal mission statement frequently. As you do, ask yourself if you are fulfilling your personal mission. Are you doing the actions that you committed to doing on a weekly, monthly, and annual basis? Pablo Picasso once said:

"Action is the foundational key to all success."

I have found this quote to be profoundly true. I could think, dream, and plan all I wanted, but it wasn't until I was willing to do the footwork, to set goals, and to take action that my life began to change. I encourage you not only to write your personal mission statement but also to share it with the important people in your life. By saying it out loud, you'll not only gain valuable support, but you will be much more inclined to follow through with your action steps.

Be aware that your personal mission statement is not written in stone, and it will change over time. It is merely an indicator of whether you are reaching your goals and dreams, and it can help keep you motivated when you feel discouraged.

BECOMING YOUR BEST

"You are capable of more than you know. Choose a goal that seems right for you and strive to be the best, however hard the path. Aim high. Behave honorably. Prepare to be alone at times, and to endure failure. Persist! The world needs all you can give."
—E. O. Wilson

We all want to function at our optimum, at our very best potential, right? So what does it mean to become your best? Becoming your best is a very personal concept, and it involves using your own yardstick to measure your progress rather than comparing yourself to others. Becoming your best means that you, in any moment, are doing the best you can do with the tools you have and that you have the willingness and desire to continue growing, changing, and learning.

You will find that the amazing life you are creating now will not only lead you to different opportunities, but it will change over time. In fact, the amazing life you are creating now may look very different from the amazing life you are creating next year, or the year after. This change is the very evolution of progress. As stated previously, your journey may be two steps forward and one step back, but steady progress and improvement always follow steady action. Here are some helpful success strategies to keep you focused and on track:

HELPFUL SUCCESS STRATEGIES:

Don't be afraid of change; rather, accept it as the one consistent fact of life. The perception of good/bad change is relative and really depends on your perspective. Don't forget that change is *always* an opportunity for growth and can be a motivator to take action.

Choose to be a lifelong learner. Keep an open mind to new ideas and consider yourself as much a follower as a leader. Closed minds gather dust, but there are endless possibilities when you keep an open mind. Study, read, listen to audio books, and go to trainings or seminars whenever possible to learn more about the topics that interest you. Spend time in your local library if money is tight. Most libraries have an audio book section and even DVD's on self-improvement and a host of other interesting topics. Make your own personal evolution a priority, and with it will come ideas and opportunities you may not have considered before.

Growth always follows the expanding of ideas and new knowledge, and once your mind has been stretched by new ideas and knowledge, it never returns to its original state. It's important to learn everything you can about being your best, whatever that best is for you.

Work hard toward the weekly and monthly and yearly goals you identified. Use your new tools every day with passion and enthusiasm and you will not fail to create your amazing life. You're no different from those who have already reached their own amazing lives; the path is similar for everyone.

When you change your negative thinking to positive thinking and take daily action to move your life forward, you'll be astonished at your results because although the process may seem slow to start, one day you'll realize that you are becoming—and have already become in many ways—the person you had only dreamt about before you knew better, before you knew that you have the power to change your life.

Trust yourself and your abilities—build and lift yourself up by honoring yourself each day through the practices of starting your day on the right foot and spending time in the special place you have designated to create your new life.

Make yourself a priority and become your own best cheerleader. Don't wait for the external clamor of recognition and acceptance to acknowledge your own brilliance. Put your wellbeing first; make sure your cup is full and you won't believe how great you feel and how much you have to share with others as a result.

Take care of yourself. Self-care is very different from selfishness. Selfishness means you are stuck on you, you, you, and that everything is about you or what you're going to get or not get out of something. Self-care is the combination of the action you take to make sure your needs are met in the different life areas that you identified for the purpose of being your best.

Make sure you get a steady diet of soul-food. Fill your soul with things that you love. Surround yourself with beauty and the things that make you feel connected to your spirit. Whether your connection is to God, the Creator, the Holy Spirit, Nature, Grandfather, flow, Jesus, Buddha, Jehovah, Allah, your Higher Self, or your angels, tap into it/him/her/them and get connected every day if possible. Connect to your source and recognize that with practice, you are becoming closer to, and developing an even stronger relationship with, the one or many that sustain your very soul. Listen intently to what you are being guided to think, do, and say. New ideas and inspiration will come to you if you're keeping an open mind.

Make a commitment to participate in your relationship with your spirit, and just like the relationships that you participate in with other people, it will bloom, flourish, and sustain you when you want or need it most. Like plugging something into an electrical socket, you can plug into your spirit each day in an effort to be present, connected, and inspired.

SUMMARY

You will find that as you work toward becoming your best, you will become a light for others. They will gravitate toward you because water seeks its own level. The healthier and happier you become in your life, the healthier and happier people you'll attract as a result. Own your power and your positivity and share it with others and it will come back to you tenfold.

When you come from this positive and productive place, you will be energized, inspired, and motivated not only to be your best, but also to pass your best on to others and like a pebble dropped into a pond, your effect on your environment will be much like the rings spreading out to all those you come in contact with. Self-care models love and respect, and when you treat yourself with love and respect, others will treat you the same. You show others through your own behavior how to treat you, and when you treat yourself with dignity and become important to you, others will naturally see that this is the way you deserve and expect to be treated.

Share your journey with others. Tell them your new story about the progress you've made, where you were, and where you are now. Whenever possible, give others hope. Hold your head high because you deserve every good thing you are manifesting in your life. These wonderful changes are a direct result of your positive thinking and the actions that you're now practicing.

Chapter 10

Creating Your Amazing Life

"Life isn't about finding yourself. Life is about creating yourself."
—George Bernard Shaw

THE BEST IS YET TO COME

Why is it so hard sometimes to believe that you deserve the very best of all things? Is it wavering faith? Is it that you struggle with low self-esteem?

When I was nine years old and things were very chaotic at home, I got a job cleaning stalls and grooming ponies at a local pony farm. In return, I got to ride the ponies after hours. I would leave the house at 6:00 a.m. and return just before dark, often coming home exhausted with dirt from head to toe. For the first time in my young life, I felt the presence of God when I spent time with those amazing creatures, and I was connected to my very spirit. I loved being around the ponies and hoped and wished for my own some day.

Around that time, my brothers were very small and my mother was in the middle of a separation from my first stepdad, but nonetheless, she knew how important the ponies were to me, and she found a way to buy me a pony of my own named Charlie. Charlie was my life and my heart. I rode Charlie from morning until night during the summers and any chance I got during the school year. We lived near Chatsworth Park in the San Fernando Valley in California during that time, so my friends and I would pack lunches and ride deep into the hills. We also gave rides to the children at a group home for disabled youth that we found on one of our many adventures. I will never forget the smiles and the delight of the kids who got to ride. I believe that was also the first opportunity I had to share something I love, something I could contribute, with those less fortunate than me.

In seventh grade, I began running with a tough crowd and getting in trouble at school, so for my own safety, I got sent to Washington State to live with my biological father for six months. I learned many important lessons during that brief time with my dad, but when I returned back home to California, my mother had sold my pony. It must have been a difficult decision for her, but when choosing food for her children or hay and boarding for the pony, the answer was clear. Nonetheless, I was devastated. There were really no words for that experience; I think I just gave up after that.

When I was twenty-four years old, a grown woman, I shared the story about Charlie with a mentor and friend. She replied, "Robin, why can't you check into getting a horse of your own or make some kind of riding arrangement with someone who has a horse? You're a grown woman; you have a job. Maybe you could find a way to get that experience back now."

I was stunned because the thought had never occurred to me, ever. Why? Because I didn't believe that I deserved anything so amazing, so wonderful, and so spirit-feeding in my life. After my years of addiction and trauma, I had forgotten that I count, that what I want is important, and that I deserve to do things and have experiences that feed my soul.

Shortly after that conversation with my mentor, I happened to be browsing through our little community newspaper and noticed an ad that read: "Half lease on a quarter horse. Please help, I am very busy at work and don't have time to ride. Call this number if you're interested. $75.00 a month, unlimited riding." I called the number and met the woman who placed the ad at her home, but more importantly, I met the horse who, by the way, was my dream horse. Had I written a description of the horse that I wanted in my wildest dreams, this would have been him. He was tall, completely jet black, and very sweet. After I signed the lease agreement, I drove as fast as I could to my mentor's house. I had horse slobber and dirt from head to toe on me, and when she saw me, she said, "What happened, Robin? How did it go?" and for the first time in my life, I broke down and cried tears of joy, pure and delicious joy. My heart was so full it felt like it was going to burst. I would've never asked for such a gift because before that moment, I didn't believe I deserved it. What a miracle and an incredible experience. I leased that horse for a while and enjoyed every minute of it until I was able to buy a horse of my own, which I did, and I rode for many, many years.

When my children were born, my horse became lonely like the horse I had leased from the woman who worked so much, so I decided he would be happier with a family who would give him the time he deserved. It was a tough day when I had to let him go, bittersweet for sure, when we found his forever home. One day, maybe I'll have another horse because I know I could have one if I choose to have one, and that I deserve to do things and have experiences that make my spirit soar!

Prior to that experience, my thoughts were so limited. My feelings of low self-worth ruled the decisions I made and the experiences I allowed myself to have or not have.

EXERCISE:

Here are some important questions to ask yourself about how you may have limited your beliefs, and how those beliefs affected your self-worth and the decisions you made in the past for your life:

Have your personal experiences or society (or both) conditioned you to believe that you're being greedy or selfish when you have high expectations for your life, or want great things and experiences for yourself?

____

____

____

____

Maybe you've tried to change something important in the past and feel that you failed, or maybe you've even succeeded and didn't know how to handle the success. Have you felt powerless and that change isn't worth the effort because it probably won't work out anyway?

____

____

____

____

____

Do you think the work involved in having what you consider a great life is too hard, or that you won't have enough time to take care of your family and your current job if you start working toward change?

____

____

____

____

____

Are you afraid of what other people may think if you actually take the plunge and start doing things differently than you have been?

____

____

____

____

____

Quit limiting yourself! Push up your sleeves, and jump into life with both feet! The only limits you have are the ones you've created. You have every single thing inside of you that you need to make the changes you're ready to make. It's time to re-evaluate your beliefs about yourself. When you begin moving toward the direction of your dreams, you will be amazed at what you are capable of!

Yes, you *will* have to work hard and make some sacrifices, but it will be worth it! Imagine what you'll accomplish and what you'll give the world when you can let those mistaken beliefs go and you become free to step-up and fill the God-given shoes that were made just for you! You deserve the best, and deep inside, you know it… the best really is yet to come!

YOU ARE THE ANSWER

"At the end of the day, all roads always and once again, lead to the place inside of you that echoes your truth. If you're not happy in this place inside meant for solace that is to be your safe harbor, then no other anchor can hold you steady. Surrender to this place inside and shine the light of reason on it. Let no one disturb you at your core so you can be free to share your peace with others."

—Robin B. O'Grady

When I was going through my separation and divorce from my husband, money was extremely tight; I was living on a dirt hill in a small manufactured home with my children, going to the food bank, and feeling utterly hopeless about my future. I remember my young son saying to me, "Mommy, someday I want to live in a house with grass" because literally there was no landscaping in our yard; it was all dirt. In all of my futility and bewilderment, I was forced to seek something inside of me, to help me move past my fear and grief and beyond my negativity.

Little did I know that what literally took me to my knees in emotional pain would be the catalyst that propelled me into my new and amazing life. I had to find the strength within me to get through this time in my life or I feared I would not be able to continue being a good mother to my children or even continue showing up for work. Yes, it was *really* that bad. The smallest thing could send me on a crying jag, and it didn't matter where I was, it just happened. To this day, I have never experienced anything as painful. I needed spiritual help and healing. I was searching for a way I could change my life when I read this passage from Neale Donald Walsch:

> It is time to move into uncharted lands. If you want to do something you have never done before, you have to do something you have never done before. If you want to go somewhere you have never gone before, you have to go somewhere you have never gone before. You cannot do something new by doing old things. If you want your life to change, you have to change your life. So go ahead. It's safe. And it's also...about time.

This passage reminded me that if I wanted change in my life, I had to be willing to walk through whatever it was that stood in my way. You can't go over obstacles, and you can't go under them—you must go through them to get to the other side.

I set up a corner of my room and began to get up twenty minutes early each morning in an attempt to get "plugged in" and to find answers to the important questions I was seeking. As I connected each day, I began to experience strength inside of me that I never knew I had. The answers to my important questions began to come to me, and my life began to change for the better quickly and profoundly.

The answers and the benevolent spirit that moves us all had been inside of me all along. All I had to do was get quiet, ask, and listen. This healing in my life was miraculous. The sun began to shine on me again, and I began to do better at work and at home. I began growing from the inside out in leaps and bounds. I have shared this story with so many people over the years who have shared similar experiences with me. To this day, meditation and prayer have been an integral and mandatory part of my life and are the foundation for starting my day on the right foot. They have become my bottom line in self-care. I crave this time now and feel off-center if I am not able to begin my day this way.

Here is the process that I practice each morning. Feel free to use mine or develop one that you are comfortable with:

- Set aside a space where you can get connected each morning (or evening if that works better for you).
- Spend 15-30 minutes in your space quietly reflecting on the day ahead, the people you love, and the things you are grateful for. See yourself moving through your day peacefully, confidently, and contently.
- Meditate (this simply means get quiet and focus) on positive feelings. Think about your blessings and how wonderful your life is. Think about being blessed with being alive in the first place. You were a winner before you were even born—you were literally one in a million in the biggest race of all, the race for your very life! You could have been anyone, but you are YOU! Ask any questions you want answered. If your mind wanders off, just gently bring it back to your original question and ask for guidance.
- It does not matter if no answers come right away; they will come with practice. Take a few breaths and a stretch and let your day begin.
- Don't forget there are three rules to meditation: perseverance, perseverance, perseverance. Just keep doing it, whether or not you feel it is working in the beginning. You will become aware over time of just how valuable this process is to your wellbeing.

All of the answers you need you can find inside of yourself. At the end of the day, you have the pen and you are literally writing the script of your life. What is it you really want? Hold still, listen, and act from that place and you will truly and surely begin creating your amazing life.

EXERCISE:

What is your self-care bottom line? What are you willing to do to get plugged in each day (whatever that means for you)?

____

____

____

____

____

If you have no interest in meditation and prayer, what are you willing to do to get plugged in each day? What feels right for you and gets you connected to your spirit?

____

____

____

____

____

When I look back now at that difficult time in my life, I am humbled and so grateful. I was on my knees figuratively and literally, and I was given exactly what I asked for and what I needed. God did for me what I could never do for myself. Now, when I look at you, I see God working in you and in your life. . Today,

I make the conscious effort to bless everyone I can—on the road, in the store, everywhere I go. I do this in my head and sometimes under my breath, but it is my way of giving back to you and the world what I have been blessed with.

NEVER GIVE UP

"Never give up, for that is just the place and time that the tide will turn."
—Harriet Beecher Stowe

Have you ever had a dream, something important you are passionate about that you wanted to manifest in your life, only to find that eventually you lose the motivation to make it happen? Maybe a few weeks or even months later, you just kind of give up on it because you get busy with other things and are distracted with day-to-day life. However, sometimes life can feel overwhelming and your tasks never-ending. Everyone needs down time to recharge and get re-inspired. It is normal to take a break from our activities, but don't give up on your dreams! Remember there is nothing you can't do if you are:

Determined, compelled, tenacious, persevering, persistent, steadfast

These are all words that describe a way of behaving and living in essence, if you truly want to live the life of your dreams. It doesn't matter that you do not feel 100 percent committed today; just take action each day anyway, and before you know it, you will be standing that much closer to the life you have always imagined. Each new day is an opportunity to change your life. If you weren't motivated yesterday, you can become motivated today.

EXERCISE:

Have you ever had a dream or a vision of something really important that you were super-motivated about, but then after a couple of weeks, you just gave up? What was the determining factor that made you decide not to follow through?

____

____

____

____

____

Did you doubt your own ability? Did you take the easy way out or get distracted by day-to-day life?

____

____

____

____

____

What will you do this time to make certain that you are committed to your dream? What are some things you can say and do when you find your determination and commitment lessening?

____

____

____

____

____

What are some affirming motivating words and statements that you can use to describe yourself? Can you use these words to gain motivation to keep moving forward when you are feeling low?

____

____

____

____

____

Do not give up on yourself, no matter what. No one can create the life of your dreams for you. It is an inside job based on the daily action you are willing to take and your own personal belief in yourself. Each day you can plant the seeds for tomorrow's harvest.

YOU'RE SURROUNDED BY OPPORTUNITIES

"The way I see it, if you want the rainbow, you gotta
put up with the rain."
—Dolly Parton

Many people have told me that their biggest challenge has been pressing through a tough situation to get to the other side, but when they were willing to stick it out and push through, the opportunity became clear. An obstacle is a barrier that blocks the action and prevents the progress or achievement of a concrete goal. Every obstacle is an opportunity either to give up and throw in the towel, or to persevere and become stronger and better, and get even closer to your goals.

An opportunity is a set of circumstances that makes it possible to do something. So what will you do today to get closer to your amazing life? What is one small action you can take to bring you closer to the reaching of your goals and to give yourself the opportunity to succeed?

When you see your obstacles as opportunities, nothing can stand in your way, and with each daily, weekly, and monthly action you take, you set up a chain of circumstances that make your dream possible. No one else can do this but you. Get up, and get going!

So many amazing people have overcome obstacles to create opportunities for themselves. Following are some of my favorite people, each introduced by one of their quotes, who have found ways to challenge their obstacles and to turn their lemons into lemonade:

"Life opens up opportunities to you, and you either take them or you stay afraid of taking them."
—Jim Carrey

Did you know that at twelve years old, Jim Carrey's father lost his job and the family was homeless and lived in a van for a while? In response, Jim got a job and worked eight hours every day after school. He speaks openly about this difficult time in his life, and he has never forgotten his roots.

"Do not be embarrassed by your failures, learn from them and start again."
—Richard Branson

Were you aware that Richard Branson, the fourth richest person in the United Kingdom and the owner of the Virgin group of brands, struggled with dyslexia and performed poorly on tests in school? His teachers assumed he would never accomplish much, but he overcame his obstacles and defied the odds.

"Although the world is full of suffering,
it is also full of the overcoming of it."
—Helen Keller

My all time favorite shero is Helen Keller. She was born in Tuscumbia, Alabama on June 27, 1880, and at the age of nineteen months, she lost her sight and hearing as a result of meningitis.

Despite overwhelming odds, with the help of her teacher, Anne Sullivan, Helen became the first blind-deaf person to communicate successfully with the sighted and hearing world.

Helen's experience gained worldwide attention. She was a highly intelligent writer and speaker, and a college graduate who focused on the amelioration of blindness. She traveled the world and was touted by Winston Churchill as "the greatest woman of our age." She also authored fourteen books and met every President of the United States from Calvin Coolidge to John F. Kennedy. She was often referred to as the "first lady of courage."

EXERCISE:

Do you know anyone who has overcome great obstacles and turned them into opportunities?

____

____

____

____

____

What do you notice about the attitudes and mindsets of people who have overcome great obstacles?

What have been some of your greatest obstacles so far? Were you able to turn them into opportunities? If so, how did you do it? What did you learn about yourself as a result?

Have you noticed that as a result of overcoming your own obstacles, you are better able to help those you love to overcome theirs?

You will need to practice the skill of breaking through your challenges. Every obstacle is an opportunity. Life is in session, and sometimes things aren't easy. In fact, sometimes life throws you curveballs—big ones you never anticipated. How you handle the curveballs when they come your way is up to you. Rather than react and take a passive role, respond and take a pro-active approach. Your response to tough times will determine your quality of life, your quality of relationships, and ultimately, your ability to succeed.

FINDING YOUR PASSION

> "You can never turn back to what or where you once were; you have stepped over the line. This is what happens when you have found your passion."
> **—Robin B. O'Grady**

Recently, as I began to realize the completion of my book after dreaming about its inception for many years, I had the experience of being full to the brim with excitement, joy, hope, and anticipation. I found it harder and harder to stop writing once I started, even when I knew I had other important tasks to take care of. I was inspired to write the following statements as a result:

> How do you know when you have found your passion? You take delight in your thoughts of it late at night when you know you should be sleeping but you just can't because you are so excited, elated, compelled to keep thinking about it as you begin to realize that your life is indeed unfolding like you've dreamt, planned, and hoped for so long.
>
> With each new day, you feel you are at the precipice, looking into your own joyful future to the degree that you live it, breathe it, sing it, become it. Your every cell is on board, and there is no more room in your heart for doubt because it is so filled with hope. You look at all the angles, examine them, try them on, then cast them away with hundreds of others, until you can see your very own creation growing, glowing, and taking on a life of own.

You feel like a rocket and are ready to break through and burst into the atmosphere to somewhere unknown, unfamiliar, but amazing. All your small thoughts and plans are behind you and you step into the grand and mighty shoes that now belong to, were made especially for, and only fit, YOU.

You have found your passion when you can't not think about it and it takes you over completely. You can feel it's arrival as surely as the rising sun like a distant, shining symphony becoming louder and clearer with each passing day until it takes over your tongue, your heart, and your very soul.

Make your passion your business. Let no one, nothing, no event or circumstance, stand in the way of your momentum. Press yourself forward and stoke your spark until it becomes a flame, then a fiery inferno for the whole world to see. Make no excuses for it, only and simply share it with others so they may, too, find their passion.

You see, my dream is no longer for sale and it feels so good! I am creating the life I have always imagined! Now it's your turn.

EXERCISE:

Ask yourself these questions:

What are you truly passionate about? If you had absolutely no limits and could do anything, what would you be doing?

____

____

____

____

What would you need to do to begin supporting the practice of your passion?

____

____

____

____

____

If you are currently working, could you keep your job and start supporting your passion on a part-time basis so as not to interfere with your current livelihood?

____

____

____

____

____

How do you suppose you would feel inside if you were actively pursuing your passion?

____

____

____

____

____

Now that you are ready and have made the commitment to pursue your passion and create your amazing life, here is some great advice I got early on from a coach: Create a two- to five-year plan (contingent upon how much action you plan on taking each day, week, month, etc.), and do **not** quit your day job until:

- You have enough money saved to pay for one full year of living expenses
- You have paid down your consumer debts
- Your new career or passion is bringing in the same annual revenue as your current job

Knowing that you are well on your way and you have a plan in place will give you great confidence, motivate you to continue moving forward, and give you hope as you reach smaller goals, knowing they will eventually lead you to the bigger picture. Go to my website at **OptimistsEdge.com** and click on the "Free Stuff" link to get a sample daily, weekly, monthly, and yearly action plan you can use to create your amazing life.

You'll be amazed as you are given new opportunities to develop your skills and continue growing. These opportunities can seem really scary at first, but each new open door is your chance to experience something new. Fear is only a feeling, and practicing courage means you're no longer shrinking away from the action you know you must take to push yourself, to keep growing, and to continue moving forward on your journey. Creating your amazing life means you have made a choice to be your best, live your best, and do your best in all of your life areas.

Your attitude is a good indicator and will now be your barometer to determine where you are on the path of creating your amazing life. If you find yourself in a bad mood, judging others, or thinking about negative outcomes, it is an indicator that you're not feeling good about yourself. You must rise above your own negative thinking and change your attitude. Remember to practice using the tools and strategies you've learned in this book. Mix and match them to determine which work best for you at any given time. They are flexible and work together in any combination. This book is your map and study guide. Don't put it on the shelf with your other books. Instead, highlight important things to remember, put sticky notes on the pages with strategies that can help you most, and read and study this book time and again.

All of the tools and success strategies I have shared with you in this book have personally and profoundly changed my life, have trained my brain to steer clear of negativity (my own and others), and have helped me continue to develop my success building skills. Similar positive changes continue to be the case for countless others I've been honored to meet, teach, and inspire over the last twenty-four years.

Your success and your amazing life are contingent upon your ability to pick up the tools laid at your feet and to use them! Do your best to keep a positive attitude regardless of the circumstances happening around you. Maintaining your positive attitude takes commitment, practice, and an ongoing awareness of your own thinking and behaviors and how each plays a huge role in your life. Tearing yourself down even in jest, and not giving yourself the opportunity to dream really big and set and meet big goals keeps you stuck in that limbo of mediocrity. On the opposite scale, building yourself up and allowing yourself, actually trusting yourself, to dream big and set big goals places you on the path of living the life you have only dreamt about up until now. Don't let your fear of failure or success keep you from the amazing life of greatness that you deserve.

Your attitude is now your personal weatherman that describes to you what is your internal climate. When something is disturbing to you or you find something wrong with someone or something, take personal responsibility because, after all, it is *your* attitude! Change your perception and you'll find that you'll begin to experience peace of mind despite the storms that life sends your way. Change your perception and those same storms may be opportunities for growth.

HAPPINESS

So much has been written about how to become happy and to find meaning and joy in your life. The truth is there is no destination "to get to." Happiness is an attitude, a mindset, and a way of life rather than the elusive feeling that so many people spend their lives looking for. Even Abe Lincoln knew this when he said:

"Most folks are as happy as they make up their minds to be."

I have discussed many tools and success strategies in this book to help you stay on the positive path, such as starting your day off on the right foot, practicing self-care, positive self-talk, meditation and prayer, and staying ever aware of your thoughts and attitude so you can choose to change the channel. While all of these tools will help you feel better physically, emotionally, and spiritually, happiness is a way of being, an internal way of functioning in the world despite external circumstances around you.

EXERCISE:

Here are some questions to consider when working toward a happy attitude or mindset:

Do you need to have the upper hand? To be right?

Are you hard on yourself and others when you or they make mistakes?

Do you find that you are secretly putting people down, judging them, or criticizing them in your head?

When you judge others, what is the immediate payoff? How does it make you feel in the long-term?

When you become aware that you are being critical in your head of others, what can you focus on instead to shift your thinking?

____

____

____

____

____

These ego-driven attitudes take away from your peace of mind, and although they may give you a temporary feeling of winning or of being superior, nonetheless, they are not in alignment with your joy.

The question to ask yourself is, "Would I rather be happy or right?" Sometimes acting in a way that is humble, in other words, not having to win, be right, or feel superior to someone else, is the path of peace. When you don't feel the need to defend yourself, cover your tracks for mistakes made, or compare yourself to others, you become less guarded and more open to feelings of happiness, joy, and contentment. When you stop criticizing and judging others covertly or overtly, you nip negativity in the bud.

Look, no one is perfect, and obviously, it's important to some degree to use discretion when determining whether you want to be around or get to know someone else. Just be mindful and spot check your own thinking. Are you being inquisitive and open-minded or judgmental and close-minded?

It is such a breath of fresh air to be free from the bondage of our own negative thinking, and when *we* are free, those around us are *also* free. When you stop correcting others, stop judging and criticizing them, they're free to express who they really are and you become a safe haven and a vessel for positive feelings.

LIGHTEN THE LOAD

"A man who is a master of patience is master of everything else."
—George Savile

When I began my journey to create my amazing life, I remember what a short fuse I had; many times I embarrassed myself with my own behavior. Little things like the long line at the bank or a flat tire could ruin my entire day, maybe even my entire week. One time in particular, I was so upset after waiting for what seemed like forever in line at the bank that I was rude and inconsiderate with the teller when I reached the front of the line. It made me feel terrible about myself, and I knew she did not deserve my negativity.

The next day, I went back to the bank with my tail between my legs and apologized for my behavior. I decided right then and there to end my pattern of "sweating the small stuff." With great effort, I began praying for patience each morning during my prayer and meditation time.

Do you know that for the next year straight, no exaggeration, I found myself at the end of every long line everywhere I went? Around the same time, one morning I heard myself loud and clear praying, "God, please give me patience." Suddenly, I realized what had happened, and I began to laugh. The whole year I had been praying for patience and God was repeatedly giving me what I had asked for—opportunities to learn how to be more patient. The long lines in the bank, at the market, they finally began to make sense. Through repetition and practice, without even being consciously aware of what had transpired, I was given patience. I got what I prayed for all right! Now, standing in line while others are fretting, sighing, and complaining, I'm the one smiling and patiently waiting my turn. By the way, I stopped praying for patience shortly after that.

When things don't go your way, and surely they won't from time to time, do you make the load heavier by contributing to the problem with negativity, or do you lighten the load and contribute to the solution by behaving with grace?

EXERCISE:

What are some things that set you off and cause you to become impatient?

____

____

____

____

Instead of becoming irritated and potentially short with others, what could you do to lighten the load for everyone involved?

____

____

____

____

____

How do you think you will benefit from taking the high road in tough situations? How will those around you benefit from you taking the high road?

____

____

____

____

FROM ZERO TO HERO

"People who dream of something bigger and better are good role models."
—**Andrew Shue**

Did you have any heroes when you were growing up, or were you your own hero? If you had no heroes, begin looking around you now. Who are the people who model the ideals, values, and personality traits you admire? What do they model that is attractive to you?

When I was in eleventh grade, I missed a lot of school for a combination of reasons. Many things were going on at home, so no one was paying attention to what I was or was not doing, and I didn't really have any guidance. Even then, I had a passion for writing, and the first mentor I can remember in my life was Mr. Campbell, my British literature teacher. He was an older man, maybe in his late sixties, who always smelled like cigarette smoke and coffee, but he had a very quick wit and would laugh often, throwing his head back and opening his mouth wide as he laughed.

I always thought Mr. Campbell was very brave, considering he was an older man at a tough school in a part of town that had so much violence that it had its own full-time police officer on duty at the school. Mr. Campbell took a lot of crap from us students, especially from those of us who really didn't want to be there. We were reading and writing essays about *Paradise Lost*, an epic poem by the seventeenth-century English poet, John Milton. I hadn't been to school for the better part of two weeks, but I had turned in my own rendition of *Paradise Lost* prior to my absence; the poem I wrote was about losing all hope after spending my life looking for paradise in all the wrong places.

When I returned back to class, Mr. Campbell had written me a lengthy note outlining in detail the strengths of my writing abilities, which he stated were clearly above average and displayed a high level of creativity. But what really stood out in my mind and my heart was that he also wrote me a paragraph of personal concern. He inquired about what could possibly be going on in my life that would cause me to miss so much school. He asked whether I was okay and whether there was anything he could do to help me. This was the first time in my life anyone had actually shown any concern or asked whether he could do anything to help me. While the class ended shortly after and I never responded to his concerns, it struck me that there were people in the world who were paying attention and who actually cared about my wellbeing and success. Though I know Mr. Campbell is long gone by now, I always wish I could have gone back and visited him to let him know how he impacted my life because surely he did.

It's so important to have someone in your life, a hero, a coach or mentor, a supporter who models the ideals, values, and personality traits that you admire. Emulating your heroes can raise the bar to help you reach your highest personal potential and give you the hope and motivation that you too can excel, succeed, and create your amazing life! So who are your heroes?

Is it the next-door neighbor who bakes homemade bread and home schools her children and still makes time to visit the elderly? Is it the man who makes it a point never to forget important dates like wedding anniversaries and birthdays? How about the woman who built a business with her bare hands and singlehandedly raised two children on her own? Is it someone who is rich and famous and able to do big things to help the world because he or she has the means?

What about when you were little? Did you have a hero growing up? Who was it and what made that person special? Begin looking around you now and you will find you are surrounded by heroes.

EXERCISE:

Who are the people who model the ideals, values, and personality traits you admire?

____

____

____

____

____

What qualities are they modeling that are attractive to you, and what similar qualities do you have?

____

____

____

____

____

Today, rather than living by default and merely getting through the next twenty-four hours, do your best to behave like your heroes. Act as if you are happy, helpful, and energetic, and you will be. Act loving, kind, patient, and tolerant, and you will be. Act successful, joyful, and as though you have unlimited abundance, and you will.

Imagine if you behaved this way, one day after another, then another, and another. Are you getting the picture? You will become what you want to be, and then maybe you will be honored to find that you already are, or have become, somebody else's hero along the way!

THE IMPORTANCE OF PERSONAL INTEGRITY

"Real integrity is doing the right thing, knowing that nobody's going to know whether you did it or not."
—Oprah Winfrey

Always do your best. When you do your best, you get to feel good about yourself. Whether you are taking out the trash or performing brain surgery, whatever you are doing, do it well.

A few years ago, while I was folding my husband and children's laundry, I started sending them love. I know this statement may sound a little odd to some people, but I find I enjoy folding laundry so much more and I do a better job when I consider who wears the clothes and how much I love them. I also spend time each morning during meditation and prayer blessing the people whose paths I will cross on that day. I think about each person I know I will see, I think about their families and what they have shared with me that is important to them, and I bless them and send them love. Everyone has his or her own challenges and triumphs. I believe we need to lift each other up in all ways whenever possible.

A bumper sticker I see all around town says, "Practice Random Acts of Kindness." I love this idea, but I choose to take it one step further. Every day, I try to do one nice thing for someone without that person finding out. If they find out, it doesn't count, so then I have to do something else. I also pick one secret thing I can do for others without getting found out on a larger scale. For instance, for a few years, I was the official toilet paper changer in every restroom I visited, literally. Public or private restrooms alike could not escape the secret wrath of my paper changing expertise. I ended up telling someone that I had been doing it, so then I chose a different task that I am not going to disclose here. I know you get the idea.

When I choose to do small kind things, I am building character. I know from the inside out what kind of person I am. I know that I am willing to go the extra mile, and by not telling others, I know my ego is not involved. Do things for the sake of being kind and helpful without getting found out and you will contribute to your own ability to remain humble.

EXERCISE:

Pick seven people for whom you can do something kind over the course of the next week (one per day). What will you do for each? Update your list weekly. (Go to **OptimistsEdge.com** for a free sample outline.)

____

____

____

____

____

____

____

Pick one task that you can contribute to for those around you without getting found out. If and when you get found out, you have to change the task to something different. For example, clean the lint screen in the dryer every day whether or not it's your laundry day. It doesn't have to be complicated, just helpful.

____

____

____

____

____

Choosing to contribute without being found out can be a great self-esteem booster because you will know in your heart of hearts that you are doing good stuff behind the scenes without any expectation or recognition. I double-dog dare you to practice this exercise regularly and see how great it makes you feel!

THE RUDIMENTS OF FAITH

"Without faith, nothing is possible. With it, nothing is impossible."
—Mary McLeod Bethune

Do you sometimes struggle with staying positive and keeping the faith when it seems like things aren't going your way? Sometimes when our faith is waning, it can be difficult to feel happy and motivated, but you can practice some simple but profound faith-building skills to help you develop the fundamental core confidence inside of you that all is well no matter what your external conditions.

Whether or not you realize it, you have faith bigger than you know! Don't believe me? Did you have faith that gravity would hold you and your surroundings to the ground this morning when you got up? Did you have faith that the sun would rise today? Have you ever gotten on an airplane expecting that it would in fact reach its destination? Do you have plans for today, tomorrow, and next week? How do you know you'll even be around?

That is faith! Having faith means that you have a strong unshakeable belief in something, or confidence in the truth, value, or trustworthiness of a person, idea, or thing. Here are some great tips for developing your faith in a more conscious and meaningful way:

- Make the choice to have faith and focus on what can be done rather than what can't. When we begin focusing intentionally on solutions rather than problems, we are no longer victims at the mercy of obstacles that show up in our way. We develop tenacity, perseverance, and emotional strength as a result. We also develop the "knowing" that no matter what comes down the pike, all will be well. This is true peace of mind and leaves no room for fear!

- Feed your faith by spending your time with like-minded people. Share time with other positive people who are proactive and supportive of your success and wellbeing. Let them lift you up, and surely, you will lift them up as well.

- Practice gratitude every day. Take time to identify and appreciate how great you already have it, the amazing people you are surrounded by, and the opportunities that you have been given. Celebrate and be thankful for your health, your loved ones, your abilities, and your many talents.

- Be a beacon of hope for others by sharing your faith, your joy, and yourself with others, especially when you are struggling with faith. When you give away what you have on the inside by serving others, you will find the sun shining on you brighter than ever!

- Practice meditation and prayer. At this point, you may be thinking this tool has become redundant and you are right! This is the glue that connects you with the life energy that animates you. You don't have to believe it, feel it, or even understand it. When you are committed to developing a relationship with whatever it is inside of you that is alive, you will find a faith beyond your wildest dreams! This faith will sustain you, motivate you, and support you in all you do.

SUMMARY

Behave in all ways as if the best is yet to come; assume that it is, and operate from the place of knowing that all good things are on their way to you. That is faith in its finest form. Make a commitment to honor yourself with the gift of time each day to get focused on and centered in the vision that you have for your life. See every challenge as an opportunity, and don't ever give up! Find your passion and share it freely with others, and you will surely continue to grow and move forward with each day that passes.

Chapter 11

Leading With Heart

"If your actions inspire others to dream more, learn more, do more and become more, you are a leader."
—**John Quincy Adams**

Inside every single one of us is a leader, whether we realize it or not, so the question is: How do *you* want to show up in the various parts of your life? Who do you want to be at work, in love and family, in social relationships, and financially? Do you want to inspire others, learn more, do more, and become more? What would that look like?

AT WORK

I decided fifteen years ago that I was going to show up for work a few minutes early each day, do the best job I could no matter the task, and keep a positive attitude to the best of my ability, mostly because it made my work more enjoyable and made me feel good about myself.

At the same time, I became very interested in leadership models and have always been a natural born leader. I began observing my coworkers' behaviors within the construct of my job at the time, and what I began to identify was astonishing! Employees who had a positive mindset naturally and with minimal effort excelled at their jobs. Not only did other employees look up to them and respect them, but employers counted on them to get the job done and felt confident that it would get done right. The cream really does rise to the top.

This realization—that a positive attitude made all the difference when it came to excelling on the job—also applied to me on a personal level. The more trustworthy and accountable I became, the more willing I was to do my job with personal and professional integrity, and the more options opened up for me with my employer. Once I made these changes, I was quickly promoted, and soon word spread about me and my efforts into the community. Because I became a servant leader, I have been able to reach and accomplish my professional dreams and aspirations and have had a very rewarding career that I would not have experienced otherwise.

EXERCISE:

How do you want to show up at your job? Even if you don't plan on staying there forever, what can you do to give your employer and coworkers your very best?

____

____

____

____

____

How has your attitude affected your employment thus far? How could showing up each day with a positive attitude improve your current job position for you and for your employer?

____

____

____

____

____

Having been the leader of several non-profit human service organizations in my career over the course of more than twenty years, I know that the best employees I have had were willing to roll up their sleeves without big egos and do whatever was asked with a positive attitude. I have many times promoted dedicated and motivated employees from within, often giving those with less education the position when they have proven to be servant leaders. These employees show up for work fully present, and at their best. They want and choose to give their best, and this behavior follows them into all areas of their lives. They lead by example and are great role models while other employees grumble through their day, doing only what is written in their job descriptions, doing the minimal tasks required at best.

AT HOME

How do you want to show up at home with your family? Stressed out after a long day of work? Your cup empty and nothing to give? Irritable and discontented? Or would you rather show up ready and able to be helpful and serve those you love most, to be a good partner to your mate, a good parent to your children, a good caretaker of your pets? If you live alone, what kind of self-care would be important, loving, and kind to create for yourself at the end of a long day?

I remember hearing someone say once that before she walked into her house at the end of each day to greet her family, she hung her worries on the worry tree. She made a conscious effort not to take the stress of her day into her sanctuary in an effort to be present and enjoy the time she had with her family. What a great metaphor!

EXERCISE:

How do you want to show up at home? What kind of leader can you be in your household?

____

____

____

____

____

What do you need to let go of at the end of the day so you can be more fully present and serve those you love most?

____

____

____

____

____

What are some things you can do to practice self-care so you can be more present for those you love?

____

____

____

____

____

QUANTUM LEAPS

"Excellence is the gradual result of always striving to do better."
—Pat Riley

As I began to create my amazing life, I decided that I was worthy of a job that would be inspiring, pay very well, and help me grow in new areas. Though I loved my job at the time, I felt that I had more than filled the shoes of my position and began to get bored. I started searching for new opportunities and found an advertised open position that seemed to meet the criteria I was looking for, a true dream job to support the creation of my new life. I meditated on the job opening each day, I fully researched the company, I reconstructed my resume, and I made the conscious declaration that the job was mine and not only was I worthy of the great job, but that the company really needed me and my expertise for the job. I bought two new suits and got a great haircut to wear to the interview for the job I knew I would receive.

I was in fact invited to interview for the position and to do a presentation for the Board of Directors, and you can bet I was ready! I showed up early (I was scared but really excited), and I met the panel of board members who conducted my interview. I was nervous, but I did a great presentation and was called back a week later for a second interview. I met with the board members once again and they hammered me with more questions. Even though I was nervous, I felt so confident that I shined from the inside out, and for the first time in my entire life, I owned my potency! I gave myself the credit and support I deserved, and I believed from my head to my toes that I was destined for greatness because I am!

Over the course of the three, yes, three interviews that I participated in, I learned all about how a successful, inspired, non-profit board functions. I learned about the importance of its strategic planning, fundraising, development processes, and many other important business practices. The board members shared as much information with me as I did with them.

As it turned out, I didn't get the position after all. For a moment, I was crushed, but with my new pair of glasses and positive attitude, how could I be disappointed when I had learned so much? I learned that if I dream big, other people take me seriously! I learned that I am worthy and capable and valuable and that I can do whatever I believe I can do! Is there a lesson bigger than that? My faith in myself has become the driving force behind the creation of my amazing life!

Shortly after I found out that I didn't get the job, I was reflecting on the experience when, suddenly, the lesson hit me like a ton of bricks! I'm supposed to water the grass where I'm standing! I am supposed to help and inspire the board of directors at my current company so *they* can transition to the next level! It is my job to keep my board growing and learning and to inspire them to serve our organization.

I learned so many important things during those interviews that I hadn't known before, and I was able to carry the information back and share it with my board of directors. Coincidentally, a salary increase came shortly thereafter because I believed I deserved it and became the person who deserved it! The point of my story here is: Don't sell yourself short with your negative thinking. Dream big and go big because you are as big as you believe you are, and remember, sometimes it's not always about you—it's about what you can bring to others. When we give our best to others, we cannot fail to grow ourselves in the process.

EXERCISE:

Are you striving to do your best or are you just getting by day-to-day and not giving your employer your best work? Either way, how do you suppose this affects your self-esteem?

____

____

____

____

____

How can always doing your best affect your current job?

____

____

____

____

____

What would your boss say about your job performance? Would he/she say that you give your employers your best work? Do you believe you are giving them your best work?

____

____

____

____

____

How can always doing your very best contribute to the creation of your amazing life?

____

____

____

____

____

Always be open to new opportunities. When a door opens, walk through it, and when a door closes, know it was meant to be. Look for the lessons and understand that every lesson counts even though it may be disguised as something completely different, so make sure to keep an open mind. Own your greatness because you *are* great. Dream big dreams and they *will* manifest. Don't be afraid of your light, but rather, let it shine like the sun. Those around you need you to lift them up, and in return, you'll be lifted up to higher heights than you can imagine. My dream, my biggest dream of all, and the creation of my amazing life is to get this book finished and to share it with you and the world! My dream is not for sale, and I don't want to settle for something *good* when I know I can reach out for something great!

"Great leaders have a heart for people. They take time for people. They view people as the bottom line, not as a tool to get to the bottom line."
—Pat Williams

From stay-at-home mom, to construction worker, to non-profit executive, we all are leaders in our own right. Leading with heart is the art of identifying and addressing, in a productive and meaningful way, the core of what is driving a person, causing a conflict, or creating discord. Over the last twenty years, I have had the opportunity to lead many teams and groups. Believe me, there were times when it was challenging, uncomfortable, and sometimes just downright irritating.

In my many administrative roles over the course of my human service career, I have had to provide constructive criticism and corrective action for employees for a myriad of reasons, and that has taught me some interesting things along the way.

First, hear people out instead of showing up with a hammer. After you state the challenge (notice I didn't say problem), learn to be a good listener and you will be amazed by how many people will take personal responsibility for their shortcomings and will find legitimate and appropriate corrective action without your intervention. This internal motivation is your best bet every time. Hearing people out also creates an atmosphere of dignity and respect. Outside forces create external motivation, and many times, temporary change, but when someone is internally motivated, changes are self-directed and tend to be permanent.

Second, listen to the feelings behind the content. People are motivated for different reasons, and they have their own perceptions. They are often driven by their feelings to react and respond in certain ways. If you can get to the bottom of who people are, you are much more likely to have influence and gain their trust and respect.

I had an employee who made a very bad decision that affected our agency and the people we serve in a very derogatory way. What she did was unprofessional and inappropriate. I was very angry and made an appointment to see her as soon as possible. In the interim, I had some time to consider the best approach. Because I was angry, I wanted to be the hammer. I knew she needed to be fired. How could she have done what she did? Didn't she know how unprofessional and inappropriate it was? Thank goodness I took some time to think about it. Here is the question I asked myself: "What would be the best approach for all concerned?"

I chose to take the high road. I knew there must have been more to the story, and after all of her hard work, I owed her the respect of hearing her out. When she came to my office, we talked about the incident that had occurred. I listened to her perception of the incident, and she also shared about some very stressful and pressing issues in her personal life that had begun leaking into her professional life. I was able to let her go kindly and respectfully, but also knowing full well that what had occurred could not be tolerated. On what could have possibly been one of the worst days of her life, I was still able to be compassionate, concerned, and kind. This approach is what I mean by taking the high road.

Leadership at its core is about building relationships. Always put your people first. When you put your people first, they will work hard for you. They will lift you up and become the very wind beneath your wings. Put tasks in second position, and if tasks are not being completed effectively, look for ways to improve the tasks rather than focusing on the person's deficiency. This people first, systems second approach is key, especially when system improvement is a priority. Many times, a new approach to your system can be the final piece of the puzzle to your organization's success, and that approach can come from the people performing the tasks who know their tasks inside and out.

I worked for a great company that had what it called a "re-engineering committee." Employees were invited to volunteer to work together at monthly meetings to look at systems that weren't producing optimum results and provide recommendations for change. When the recommended changes produced results that benefitted the organization monetarily, the re-engineering committee members involved got to split a portion of the profit or money saved. Quarterly, the employees would receive a check (sometimes a big one!) for their contributions to the committee, but even more importantly, they felt invested in the company because they knew their opinions were important, and that they had a personal investment in the company's improvement. What a great idea!

Sometimes it can be difficult to get people on the same page, especially when they are passionate about something. Some simple strategies to practice when problem solving and helping others to work through conflict and discord are:

- When you have to confront an employee with an issue, whenever possible, sleep on it before deciding to address it, especially when you are tired, angry, or confused and need clarity about a situation. After a good night's sleep, meditate about the best possible solution.

- Put down the hammer. Coming in hard with a hammer, a closed mind, and an agenda never resolves a problem. But also remember to make a decision and make it quickly but kindly. Waiting too long to make a tough decision can create considerable damage to the organization and those you serve.
- Be a good listener. What is someone *really* trying to tell you? Is he or she hurt? Angry? Sad? What is underneath the conflict?
- Honor it! You don't have to agree with someone's perception or perspective, but acknowledge the other person's truth. Right or wrong, it's true to them.
- Give honest feedback, including constructive criticism, but be sure to follow the criticism by also identifying strengths. Everyone has strengths, so point them out.

You catch more flies with honey every single time, and treating people with compassion, listening to what they have to say, looking for the meaning behind the words, and problem solving together create an atmosphere of trust, harmony, and inclusion that is empowering and respectful, and after all, don't we all want to be empowered and treated with respect?

CONSTRUCTIVE CRITICISM

"Every human being is entitled to courtesy and consideration. Constructive criticism is not only to be expected but sought."

—Margaret Chase Smith

Part of personal development involves being willing to take constructive criticism. Many people over the years have told me constructive criticism is a sore spot for them, and a very difficult thing to be open-minded about, especially when they have low self-worth to begin with. Part of the problem is that some people take constructive criticism as a personal affront or cut-down. Other people have no interest in hearing what you believe they should improve.

Personally, while sometimes it is difficult for me to listen to constructive criticism, I have also found it invaluable when identifying my blind spots or where my ego is bigger than life. One example is that a few years ago I had to do a speech for a group of people whom I respected and admired. A good friend and professional from my community attended the event and was seated next to me prior to the speech.

After my speech, she commented on some areas of improvement that I could use. At first, it hurt my feelings because I struggled with nervousness prior to the event, and I thought she was being somewhat unsupportive at the time, but on a larger scale, it pushed me to join Toastmasters International, which is a reputable worldwide speech club that helps people develop their public speaking and professional skills. As a result of my friend's comments and my membership at Toastmasters International, I have grown so much as a speaker and a professional. That never would have happened if I had not been able to listen to and consider what my friend said after my speech that day. Sometimes, others can identify our blind spots, and if they are brave enough to let us know what they see, it can be very valuable information.

On the opposite hand, don't take constructive criticism too seriously. If you feel that it relates, great. If it doesn't, then let it go. Some people are just super-critical, and they are the first to point out what they perceive to be the weaknesses of others. These are usually people who feel bad about themselves and put others down to try and make themselves feel better.

EXERCISE:

Do you feel open to someone giving you constructive criticism?

____

____

____

____

____

If not, can you at least see the value in being open to it?

____

____

____

____

____

One of the best ways I have found if you have constructive criticism to give someone else is to ask first: "Can I give you some constructive criticism?" That's a great way to start.

UNCONDITIONAL REGARD

Have you ever had a relationship with someone and just felt completely accepted by him or her? You knew that it didn't matter if you made mistakes, said something wrong, or weren't at your best because you knew that this person loved you for you, imperfections and all. Maybe it was a grandparent or close friend, or if you were super-blessed, maybe it was a significant other like your husband or wife. Didn't you feel supported and like you could take on the world because you knew this person believed in you?

Sometimes our own expectations about ourselves and others can ruin the simple beauty that occurs when we are free just to be ourselves. Likewise, when we accept others as they are, they feel free to be themselves without judgment, and who are after all, to expect or tell other people what they should be, have, or do?

A wise friend told me once that if you can't accept how someone is today, you may as well walk away because you can't expect others to change in the ways that you dictate. Being disappointed because someone doesn't realize what you perceive as his or her "potential" means that you have put yourself in the position to judge another and that you think you know what is best for someone else. Potential comes from the inside out and is measured by the way you feel about. Your potential and the reaching of your potential is measured by!

When you accept others as they are and let go of your expectations, you become a magnet, and you are in the position to support and be of maximum help and service to another. *Never let anyone convince you that you are not good enough. We are all, everyone, stronger than we know.*

SUMMARY

Be a leader wherever you are standing—at work, at home, and in life. Do your best to be your best and you will show up in your relationships as the best version of yourself. There is always more to learn, so keep an open mind. If you can be open to constructive criticism, you can use it as a stepping stone for growth.

Give others the space to be imperfect and allow them to be just who they are. You will find in the process that you are much more gentle and loving, not only to them but to yourself.

Chapter 12

The Five Star Success System©

"To say yes, you have to sweat and roll up your sleeves and plunge both hands into life up to the elbows. It is easy to say no, even if saying no means death."

—Jean Anouilh

Your amazing life is contingent upon your ability to assimilate, internalize, and consistently practice the five following principles of success: Dream, Plan, Act, Serve, and Achieve. These five principles are the clay that you will mold into the foundation that will be your amazing life. The degree to which you are able to embrace, internalize, and consistently practice these powerful and timeless universal principles will determine your ability to create a life filled with passion, true contentment, peace of mind, and the power to move mountains, which before, you may have never considered possible.

In previous chapters, you identified your negative thinking habits, the behaviors that have kept you stuck in the past, and how to let go of self-defeating patterns that contribute to a poverty mindset like negative feelings, fear, low self-worth, resentment, and difficulty coping with change. You have learned to turn your greatest adversities into your biggest assets and how to begin telling your new story, and you have clearly identified the areas in your life that you would like to change and how you will specifically make those changes. Now it is time to set all the bricks in place and make a commitment to yourself to fill the shoes that were made just for you and have been waiting for you all along.

STAR ONE: DREAM

"If one advances confidently in the direction of his dreams, and endeavors to live the life which he has imagined, he will meet with success unexpected in common hours."
—Henry David Thoreau

What have you found out that you truly want in your life as a result of reading this book and practicing the tools and strategies you've learned so far? What does the life of your dreams look like? You must find a way to be able to see yourself and your dreams fulfilled. You must see it in order to be it. We discussed starting your day on the right foot by setting aside a place or a space if you will—somewhere you can give your complete focus and attention to what it is you really want and to ask important questions about your life and receive valuable clarity and guidance. Now we will take it a step further.

Your assignment is to create a collage or vision board that contains a tangible picture of your dream. You can use a blank wall, a cork board, a large poster board, whatever you have available to begin creating the visual picture of what you will create in your life. As you go through the normal course of your day out in the world, begin noticing things you like. At work, on the road, in the store, just notice things you like. The pretty smile of the lady at the bank, the color of the trees on your way home, the sound of the wind blowing, the new car in the parking lot at the grocery store, whatever it is. As you begin noticing what you like over the course of your ordinary day, also notice how these same things begin presenting themselves to you more and more frequently. Express gratitude as you notice these things more often. Your positive and grateful attitude will open the door and attract to you the very things you seek. The more you practice this attitude, the more often what you like will be presented to you.

Start collecting pictures of what you like from magazines, family photos, newspaper articles, or other meaningful items, such as quotes from your favorite personal development book. My own vision board contains pictures from magazines such as travel magazines, business magazines, excerpts and quotes from self-development books, pictures of me and my family in places we have traveled already and experiences we have had together, and pictures of places I will go one day. I have pictures of the people I love, local newspaper articles about the programs I've created in my community, and pictures of my wonderful team. I also have a small collection of prayer totems I keep nearby and a whole stack of miscellaneous personal development books that I have counted on to guide, direct, and steer me on my path over the years.

Another example from my collage is a picture from a magazine of a beautiful watch encrusted with diamonds. A few years ago, I decided I would begin collecting beautiful watches, as I did not own a watch at that time and have never really been a jewelry wearing type person, though I do appreciate beautiful jewelry. I put a picture of my dream watch on my collage, and within six months, I was wearing that exact watch. When I bought my dream watch, I took its picture off my collage and replaced it with a picture of a different and very beautiful watch. I have no doubt that I will have that watch very soon. I also put on my collage pictures of my book cover, of someone who looks like me signing books for a crowd of people, and pictures of me that were taken during my speaking engagements to help me continue with and grow my coaching and speaking career, which has become one of my biggest passions.

Another picture I posted on my collage is of a door with a VIP star on it. Each day during my morning meditation, I looked at the picture and thought, "One day I will indeed finish my book and have opportunities to share my message on a larger scale," but I didn't really specify how the door with the star on it would manifest itself into my life. One morning last year, I was putting the key into my office door at work when I happened to glance up at my nameplate on my door. I literally got goose bumps when I realized someone had put a VIP star on my office door! It was identical to the star on my vision board. Can you believe it? I have no idea where it came from, but I do know it was a direct result of my focused and positive vision manifesting into reality.

When I experience the manifestation of something that I have put on my collage, I take it down and put it in the pile of places, things, and experiences that have already manifested, and I replace it with something new. Over time, my "already manifested" pile has gotten bigger and bigger and has become my biggest motivator and source of inspiration.

Create your collage with pictures of what you will achieve in your life. This is the time to go big! Remember, there are no limits except the ones you place on yourself. If you could do anything, what would it be? What is your passion? What fills your emotional, spiritual, and physical cups to the brim? What unique talents do you have to share with the world?

If you love to travel, use pictures of places you will go. If you want more money, use pictures of money and experiences that you hope to have that reflect financial abundance. If it is more love and joy you are seeking, use pictures that represent loving relationships, families, and joyful people and experiences. If you would like better health, use pictures of healthy food, people working out, whatever your definition of better health looks like. If you're interested in writing a book or being a professional speaker or leader in your community, use pictures of bestselling books, or leaders and speakers you will emulate. Make a sample book cover of the book you will one day publish and add it to your collage.

Spend 20-30 minutes each day looking at your pictures, reviewing your dreams and goals, and practicing gratitude as you begin manifesting the experiences and things you have placed on your collage. As you feel the feelings of these amazing opportunities manifesting in your life, express your love and gratitude. Recognize that you are blessed and that you are once and for all finally creating your amazing life! Remember, what you think about, you bring about! Your focused attention and time will help you fine tune your vision of what it is you really want in your life and how you will get it.

Your collage is not written in stone. As time goes on, you may want to take your collage down to reorganize and restructure it. I find myself updating my collage usually once or twice a year, contingent upon what has changed in my life and in my heart. My collage looks very different today than it did five years ago. Your collage should be a visual guidepost and daily reminder that you have a new purpose, new hope, and a new way of living that will indeed bring you what you ask for. This new daily practice takes discipline, but it is worth its weight in gold! It's easy to get in the habit of hitting the ground running once your day begins, but by slowing down long enough to get centered, focused, and inspired at the beginning of each day, you will get connected with yourself in a way you may have never been connected before. You will be clear, focused, driven, and centered. Eventually with practice, you will grow to crave this time each day, and it will become paramount in the reaching of your goals.

Let me add one more thing that has helped me so much in the realization of my dreams: Let your last thought each night be on your dream, and upon awakening, let your dream be the first thing on your mind. This focus will help you realize your dream on a subconscious level as you go to sleep, and it will help you always begin your day with the daily intention of reaching your dreams. Live and breathe your dream. Think about it often. Imagine in your mind's eye what it looks like, what you'll look like, what you'll feel like as your dreams become reality. But a dream with no plan is only a dream. You must know clearly and precisely what footwork you need to complete to begin moving in the right direction. A boat without a rudder is lost at sea.

STAR TWO: PLAN

"A straight path never leads anywhere except to the objective."
—Andre Gide

In the last section, you literally and specifically identified what your amazing life looks like, you made a commitment to give yourself time each morning to cultivate your dream, and you gave yourself permission to live your dream. Now it is time to plan out precisely how you will make it happen. To plan is to create a list of action steps or a method worked out by hand that contains the timing and resources used to achieve your objective. Simply stated, to plan is to move or take action. On my website at **OptimistsEdge.com**, you will find a free planning guide to help you write-out your specific and measurable goals because there is something that happens between the heart and the pen that just doesn't happen between the mind and the mouth. When you have a tangible plan in your hands, it is an internal call to action. Go to the website and click on free tools to get your printable planning guide.

EXERCISE:

In the meantime, here is an overview of how to formulate a plan:

What are your top three goals?

1. Goal Number One: (Example: My goal is to write an ebook outlining how to help others excel in a professional environment.)

____

____

____

2. Goal Number Two: (Example: My goal is to market this ebook on the Internet.)

____

____

____

3. Goal Number Three: (Example: My goal is to begin speaking about my book at local networking meetings to market further my ebook and increase Internet sales.)

____

____

____

Now that you are clear about your top three goals, let's break them down to identify what specific action needs to be taken in order to meet them successfully. According to this particular plan, your timeline for completion is one year. You can complete it in a variety of ways, such as: one hour of daily work Monday through Friday, five hours of work sometime over the weekend, or attendance at a two-hour webinar each month and a speaking engagement for approximately thirty to sixty minutes once a month.

Goal One: (Example: Write an ebook.)

Daily Action: (Example: Spend twenty minutes a day researching professionalism in the workplace and building an outline for my ebook.)

____

____

____

____

____

Weekly Action: (Example: Spend three hours weekly developing my ebook content according to what I have found out during my research.)

Monthly: (Example: Complete one of twelve chapters of my ebook.)

Yearly: (Example: At the end of year one or sooner, my ebook will be complete.)

Goal Two: (Example: Market my ebook on the Internet.)

Daily Action: (Example: Spend twenty minutes a day learning Internet marketing skill building.)

Weekly Action: (Example: Spend one hour weekly researching other Internet marketers and how they are marketing their ebooks.)

____

Monthly: (Example: Attend one Internet marketing webinar for two hours.)

Yearly: Example: (At the end of year one or sooner, build a free website to begin marketing my ebook.)

Goal Three: (Example: Begin speaking about my book at local networking meetings to market further my ebook and increase Internet sales.)

Daily: (Example: Spend twenty minutes researching local networking meetings and service groups for potential speaking opportunities.)

____

____

____

____

____

Weekly: (Example: Spend twenty minutes making phone calls to secure dates to begin speaking at networking meetings and service groups.)

____

____

____

____

____

Monthly: (Example: Speak at one service meeting per month/approximately 30-60 minutes.)

____

____

____

____

____

Yearly: Review

Can you see how simple achieving your goals becomes when you have a plan of action? Even if you have a full-time job already, just setting a small amount of time aside each day, week, and month will help you move forward. Consider ways you can make time for these activities a priority. It may be that you have to let some other things go or adjust your schedule slightly to make sure you have time. For instance, if you watch TV, maybe you can limit the time you spend watching, or if you usually exercise in the evening, maybe you could instead get up earlier, exercise in the morning, and designate time in the evening to meeting your goals. If you have children at home, maybe you could do your research and writing after the kids go to bed or you could do your homework while they are doing theirs.

I will tell you that while working full-time and also going to online college full-time for my business management degree, with two teenage boys at home, I was able to complete this book and build my coaching and speaking business, but it wasn't always easy. I was never a big fan of TV, so that wasn't a challenge, but I am often the first one up in the morning and the last one to go to bed at night. I can also tell you that it has been worth every minute of time I have spent, and with each goal I have realized, I have become more energized, more inspired, and more hopeful and passionate about the work I love so much. I would also like to add that my children are my number one priority. I haven't had to sacrifice my relationship with my children to build my business. I am still available to hold down my household, tuck my children in at night, and to maintain a good relationship with my husband. I also look forward to and plan on working full-time from home very soon, and I know when the time comes, it will all have been worth it and I will be ready! If I can do this…you can too!

STAR THREE: ACT

"There are risks and costs to action. But they are far less than the long range risks of comfortable inaction."
—John F. Kennedy

You are now at the jumping off place because you are at the point where physical action is necessary. Here is where your behavior will either initiate permanent and lasting change or you will sink back into the patterns you have known for so long. Will you jump headlong with both feet into your new life and say, "Yes" to the creation of your amazing life, or will you succumb to mediocrity and settle for less than your true calling, living your life by default and moving in whatever direction the wind is blowing? This is the fork in the road. Come join me and countless others who have made it to the other side. Once and for all, say, "Enough is enough," and take the plunge. Roll up your sleeves and let's get busy!

Here is a note I wrote myself when I, once and for all, made the decision to move full-steam ahead:

> Note to Self: You will need to be brave! When all the other fish around you are swimming downstream, you will need to swim up. You must gather your gumption, your dreams, and your hope, and mix them all together until they become a tornado, a driving force. This can only be done one day at a time, one thought and action at a time, but the synergistic effect will support and propel you into the good life...the life of your dreams. Go for it and don't give up no matter what!

You have a dream, you have a plan, and now you must complete the action steps of your plan. As you are doing your research each day, you will begin to find others with similar dreams who have taken action and found success. Study them and find out how they did it. What did they do, and where did they go to connect to others with similar interests?

If you are an aspiring author, speaker or coach, where do those with similar interests and goals meet to connect with one another in your community and in the online community? Whatever your goals and aspirations, make arrangements to begin connecting with like-minded people through local networking groups, seminars, personal development workshops, and even webinars, many of which are cost free. Let people know who you are, what your plans are, and ask a lot of questions.

You will be pleasantly surprised to find that most people and networking groups are open to meeting and sharing their information with you about how they've achieved their goals. They will also take you seriously. They know through personal experience that you can achieve your goals and live your dreams. They have done it and they believe you can do it too. The pinnacle of empowerment is to begin realizing that you can and will achieve your goals and to get closer and closer with each passing day to the realization of your dreams; to see them begin to manifest as a result of your hand in your life is a feeling that no employer, no external person, place, or thing can give you. This is living with passion! This is what it feels like and looks like when you are creating your own amazing life!

I can't express enough that the number one biggest gift I have ever given myself was to get a coach. As a result of my open mindedness and willingness to let someone else into my dream, I was given resources, support, and encouragement that I never would have been able to muster on my own. At an accelerated pace, I was able to develop fully this book, to gain invaluable speaking and coaching opportunities, and to begin building my business with an entire group of like-minded people supporting me every step of the way. It has been a fantastic journey, and I have not had to reinvent the wheel because I've been willing to stand on the shoulders of other great people who have already walked the path and found success.

If you are interested in coaching services, I would love to walk with you on your journey. You don't have to go it alone, and I can help you accelerate your plans and success. Go to **OptimistsEdge.com** for more information about my coaching services via my Dream Team Coaching Services.

Take action each day. Let no day pass from here on out without honoring your dream by taking at least one small action. If by some chance you skip a day, let it go and get back into action the very next day. Sometimes life gets super busy, but do not let it distract you indefinitely from your plans and goals.

Keep your forward momentum and the synergy will continue to propel you along. Your success is contingent upon your commitment to your dream, the following of your plan, and your ability to stay focused and positive. Times will be hard, and sometimes, it may seem like you will never realize your dream. During these times, you will need to break through your negativity and fear to be your own biggest cheerleader. Change the negativity channel in your head. Nothing, no one, no circumstance or person, can deter you from creating your amazing life. Use your collage as a guide and a motivator.

Please know also that there will be many people around you who don't understand what you are doing. Maybe they're afraid of change themselves or afraid that what you're doing may change the nature of your relationship with them. Understand they have their own set of fears and beliefs. Other people, maybe even family members and good friends, may not agree with or support what you are doing. They may tell you it can't be done and to come back to reality. This advice is unfortunate and may hurt your feelings, but it doesn't need to change what you're doing. Everyone has his or her own row to hoe. When you (and they) begin to experience the benefits of reaching your goals, they will have a better understanding of what you are doing and why. Let them be who they are, but don't let it deter you from being who you are. Misery loves company even when it comes to family and loved ones, so remember not to put the jacket on. It doesn't fit you, it smells bad, and it's not your style! You need to build your self-worth and positivity muscles and be okay with others not approving of you.

One time I and a psychiatrist I worked with closely in my career were discussing the temperament that human beings are born with. His description was very eye-opening, and I have often used his analogy over the years:

> Many people are like beer steins while others are like wine glasses. If you slam a wine glass onto a table, what happens? It shatters. But what happens when you slam a beer stein onto the table? It withstands the pressure. Learn to be the beer stein! When people slam you, be tough enough to withstand it; begin developing the attitude that what others think of you is none of your business!

Gain support from those who do believe in you and what you are doing! In relation to your dreams, plans, and goals, stick with those who understand and support you. Gaining support is another great reason to connect with like-minded people, networking groups, and a coach. It is so empowering to find those who have been where you are going and are excited and more than willing to share their experiences with you because they have been right where you are! They know the value of serving others and do so generously because someone took the time to be of service to them when they needed it most! I don't know where I would be today without the safety net of my coach and the many people I have met through networking who have lifted me up, supported me during my toughest times, and have infused my process with a continuous supply of hope and inspiration!

You will need to practice discipline by making time for daily action, by following your written plan, and by connecting with others. Action will indeed be the touchstone to your progress from here on out. It will bring you to the Fourth and most powerful success principle of all: To Serve.

STAR FOUR: SERVE

"Whoever renders service to many puts himself in line for greatness—great wealth, great return, great satisfaction, great reputation, and great joy."

—Jim Rohn

In the last section, we determined that you will need to take clear and decisive action and develop new and consistent habits to continue successfully moving forward. You will need to gather moral reinforcement and support by seeking others who have been where you are going, and you will also need to toughen up and be less sensitive because some people won't support you or understand what you're doing because they don't know any better. You will need to learn how to handle rejection, and when you can accomplish this, you will become unstoppable.

People will naturally begin to gravitate toward you because of your newfound confidence and will count on you to lead the way, provide direction and support, and to help them get where *they* want to be. When people gravitate toward you, it is the ultimate honor and privilege because when we give away what we have been given, the rewards of our selflessness come back to us tenfold. Do not pass up the opportunity to help someone else. Nothing is more rewarding than knowing you have something to share with others, and nothing is more empowering than the realization that you are now experiencing the fruits of your labors.

"Try to help others. Consult their weaknesses, relieve their maladies; strive to raise them up, and by so doing you will most effectually raise yourself up also."
—Joseph Barber Lightfoot

As you find the ability to be of maximum service to your fellows emotionally, professionally, and monetarily, you have an opportunity and, I believe, an obligation to share of yourself and your resources to lift others up.

There are no limits to serving others because God will work through me, as me, to help me achieve my dreams in a way that helps others for the greatest good. In this way, I feel I can give myself completely to the world, and I will be put where I can be of maximum service to all at all times. I worry less about the events of the world and think more about what I can contribute to make the world a better place. This shift in thinking has decreased my anxiety about yesterday, tomorrow, and the future, and it has given me unshakable confidence and faith in the path that lies before me.

In the same way that the wave is connected to and part of the ocean, you are a part of God. Wherever you are standing is holy ground. Own this truth within yourself—that you are indeed a piece of God—and begin to focus on seeing God in everyone you meet. Let go of petty and worldly worries and find the freedom you are meant to experience in this lifetime. You are so much more than your current circumstances; we are all equally magnificent pieces of God!

YOUR RESPONSIBILITY PLEDGE

What do you have to offer someone else? What is it you want to contribute to the world? What kind of a legacy do you want to leave for your family, friends, and those most in need? I developed an exercise called the Responsibility Pledge which is a great way to get in touch with how, what, and who you will serve as you navigate your way to your amazing life. Here is an example of a Responsibility Pledge from a prior coaching client. Notice she used "I" statements frequently to reflect that she is taking personal responsibility for the mark she plans to leave on those she loves and the world as a result of serving others:

> From this day forward, I am a messenger of hope and inspiration. I educate, empower, and inspire others to succeed in love, life, money, and work. My life is a declaration! I am intention-

ally compelled and passionate about helping others, reaching my dreams for myself and my family, and leaving my children and the world an incredible legacy, and as I follow my dreams, I am more successful than I ever imagined. Thank you, thank you, thank you.

My suggestion to her was that she memorize her pledge, and post it in several places as a reminder. Notice, she expressed gratitude at the end of her pledge, internalizing and allowing it to be true for her as though it had already happened. If you can visualize yourself achieving all that you are working toward as though it has already happened—if you can see it, touch it, taste it, hear it, and smell it—you will surely live it.

Creating your responsibility pledge is an incredibly powerful process that can help you through the most difficult times. If you go to my website **OptimistsEdge.com** and click the "Free Stuff" button, you will find a sample pledge certificate that you can use to make your own Responsibility Pledge.

Serving others is also a great contributor to positive self-worth. If you have something that someone needs (your listening ear, your time, your experience, money, whatever it is), then give it freely whenever you can. Again, what you give comes back to you. Notice and be grateful when you experience this cycle, grateful that you have something to give, grateful for all you have already, and grateful for everything you are receiving.

Call a friend who has been struggling (not the one who held you hostage with his or her constant negativity), donate time at your local pet shelter, or be a reading buddy at your local elementary school. Some other benefits of serving others include:

- Feeling that you have purpose and meaning in your life
- Increased self-worth
- Increased connections in your community
- Improving your community and society as a whole
- The feeling that you have something to contribute to the world
- Great role modeling for others

When you discover the value of being of service to someone else and make it a regular part of your life, you know that you are living for greatness. Serving others is selflessness in its best form and it feels great!

STAR FIVE: ACHIEVE

"The starting point of all achievement is desire."
—Napoleon Hill

Your heart's desires are on their way to you. You are writing the script of your life each day through your thoughts and behaviors, whether positive or negative. You are in essence the only catalyst or deterrent from the creation of your amazing life. What you do now will determine the very outcome of your life. As you look at your collage and your Responsibility Pledge each day, and as you follow and achieve the action items on your plan, you will begin to realize that you can and are indeed creating your new and amazing life. As you recognize and express gratitude for the materialization of your dreams, you will find your desire, inspiration, and motivation to continue to push forward are growing in leaps and bounds.

You have already made the effort to clear out the emotional clutter that has kept you stuck, and you have a new pair of glasses from which to see your future and the world. You can now begin to accomplish things you never believed you could prior. Like a snowball that gets bigger and bigger as it rolls downhill, your process, your experience, will continue to be the fuel that fires your forward momentum.

You will find yourself receiving new opportunities that seem to come from nowhere. The right people will be placed in your path at the right time. All the resources you need will present themselves along the way, and you will be amazed as you recognize and own that you are creating your life. Yes, it has been you all along. No more excuses. You are what you believe you are, and your current life is a reflection of your previous thoughts and behaviors. So what will your future look like?

Mountainous obstacles and challenges that would have put you out of the game before are now only molehills. English nineteenth century author Thomas Carlyle once said:

> "Nothing stops the man who desires to achieve. Every obstacle is simply a course to develop his achievement muscle. It's a strengthening of his powers of accomplishment."

From this moment forward, let nothing stand in the way of you and your dream. Expect to succeed and surely you will. Let go of your mental negativity and release the negativity of others. Continue using this book like a study guide. Read it again and again, and as you do, you will continue building *your* achievement muscles. Highlight sections that have the most meaning for you. Notice that each time you pick up this book, you find a different jewel you never noticed before. Share your findings with others who are on the same path. Use my Five Star Success System: Dream, Plan, Act, Serve, and Achieve, and you will manifest more love, more joy, better health and relationships, and more abundance than you could have ever imagined. End the day thinking about and visualizing your dream and begin the day on the right foot with meditation and prayer and with hope in your heart.

"I arise full of eagerness and energy, knowing well what achievement lies ahead of me."

—Zane Grey

SUMMARY

Dream your biggest dream. Go Big! The only limits you have are the ones you place on yourself! Let no person, excuse, or circumstance stand in your way. Plan your success by writing it out clearly and acting on it. Add to and modify your plan over time and take action daily. Seek out and serve others every chance you get. Lean on them and help them reach their goals also. You can't keep what you have without giving it away. You will find yourself standing at the gates of success, whatever success means for you, and you will indeed create your amazing life. You will achieve your heart's desire and so much more as you move beyond negativity and practice optimism in all of your worldly affairs.

In closing, I want to leave you with some challenges to inspire and motivate you as you continue moving forward. Read them, post them where you can see them, memorize them, and share them with others on your path:

1. I challenge you now to make your own dreams and aspirations the most important thing in your life.
2. I challenge you to let go of the poverty and scarcity mindset and tell yourself often: "I am so blessed and grateful for what I have. All my needs are being met and I have unlimited abundance in my life."
3. I challenge you to be aware of your own negativity and to change the channel in your head to something positive.
4. I challenge you to release the negativity of others and of the media. Focus on what is positive and good in your life and in the world.
5. I challenge you to turn your coal into diamonds and to look for the silver lining in every situation.
6. I challenge you to let go of worry and fear and replace them with thoughts of achievement and success.
7. I challenge you to forgive others, let go of your past, and begin telling your new story.
8. I challenge you to roll with change and use every challenge as an opportunity for self-development.
9. I challenge you to seek out others who can help you and to serve others whenever you are able.
10. I challenge you to use the tools and strategies in this book to create your amazing life. Write out your plan, begin taking action, and get a coach to accelerate and support your new life.

For twenty-five years, I have been creating my amazing life. Join me and so many others as we continue the path toward our dreams. Don't forget to acknowledge and enjoy the successes along the way, and as you move forward, I have one final challenge for you:

"Optimism is the faith that leads to achievement. Nothing can be done without hope and confidence."
—Helen Keller

I challenge you to practice optimism to the very best of your ability from this day forward. Perhaps I can help you get the *Optimist's Edge*. I hope you will contact me to share your thoughts, dreams, and goals. Welcome to your new amazing life. I have been waiting for you, and I'm so glad you are finally here!

Thank you and God bless you.

Your friend,

Robin O'Grady

Robin B. O'Grady

About The Author

Robin O'Grady is an author, professional keynote speaker, publishing coach, and Internet entrepreneur. She believes that we are all capable of achieving individual and organizational success when we *"Dream, Plan, Act, Serve, and Achieve."* Robin O'Grady has inspired thousands of audiences over the last twenty-five years to move beyond their challenges and create the lives of their dreams. Today, she is known for her Five Star Success Strategy by high-achievers nationwide.

Robin is the founder of several programs in her community: O'Hana House, The Lighthouse, and Forward Bound. These programs provide stable housing and supportive services for low-income chronically homeless individuals and families. After facing and overcoming several challenges in her own life, including the trauma and post-traumatic stress disorder associated with domestic violence, poverty, and addiction, she has used her experiences as a catalyst to inspire, motivate, and help others do the same. Robin was the 2013 recipient of the Soroptimist International Ruby Award and has been profiled in the *Kitsap Sun*, the *Bremerton Navigator*, and on Service Above Self Radio. To date, Robin's genuine love and passion for people and her ability to inspire others have helped hundreds of her clients to change their lives and achieve their professional and personal goals with stunning results.

Originally from California, Robin graduated from California State University Dominguez Hills with her counseling certification in 1992. She and her husband live in Port Orchard, Washington with two teenage boys, Jesse and Gavin. For more information about Robin O'Grady, visit www.OptimistsEdge.com.

Coaching Services

Robin O'Grady has been successfully guiding and inspiring others since 1988. Her unique coaching style and her Five Star Success System provides an effective roadmap for permanent change and success. Robin's experience spans more than twenty-five years, over which time she has helped many hundreds of people change their lives forever. Robin's Dream Team Coaching Program includes one-on-one coaching, weekly conference calls, and personal mentoring directly from Robin O'Grady. She also provides ghostwriting services to those who are interested in writing their own books and prefer assistance with the technical skills of writing. She also offers her Dream Team Institute to all of her coaching clients, which occurs over the course of a transformational weekend at different locales several times per year.

Book Publishing Coaching:

Robin's unique road map will take your visions and inspiration and turn them into a published book within 6-18 months. Your book will then be a lead-generating tool to serve as your platform that will help grow your speaking, coaching, and consulting practice.

Speaker Coaching:

Robin's experience as a professional speaker gives her the knowledge to help you build a speaking career. She will share with you her speaking formula that will help keep your speaking calendar full.

Life Coaching:

Robin's twenty-five years of experience helping others identify and overcome their barriers to create amazing and successful lives makes her the expert.

For a 30-minute, complimentary consultation, contact:

www.OptimistsEdge.com

Book Robin O'Grady to Speak

When it comes to choosing a professional speaker for your next event, you'll find no one more respected or inspirational—no one who will leave your audience or colleagues with such a renewed passion for life—than Robin O'Grady, one of the most gifted speakers of our generation. Since 1988, Robin has delivered more than 1,000 inspirational presentations.

Whether your audience is 10 or 10,000, in North America or abroad, Robin O'Grady can deliver a customized message of inspiration for your meeting or conference. Robin understands your audience does not want to be "lectured" but rather is interested in hearing stories of inspiration, achievement, and real-life people overcoming their challenges to create success.

As a result, Robin O'Grady's speaking philosophy is to humor, entertain, and inspire your audience with passion, genuineness, and stories proven to help them achieve amazing results. If you are looking for a memorable speaker who will leave your audience wanting more, book Robin O'Grady today.

To see a highlight video of Robin O'Grady and find out whether she is available for your next event, visit her site below. Then contact her to schedule a complimentary pre-speech interview by phone:

www.OptimistsEdge.com

robinogrady@wavecable.com

(360) 731-2313